PRAISE FOR *SAIL THE 7 CS WITH MICROSOFT EDUCATION*

Ahoy! Becky and Kathi are true changemakers and have provided an informative and engaging resource for educators. Preparing students to chart a course for their future in the modern workplace requires a focus on unleashing and developing skills. We need to build creative, collaborative, critically thinking learners who can effectively embrace technology and communicate their vision and passion to others. Most of all, we need to build a culture of compassion to enable students to apply their talents to helping others. While many valuable Microsoft technologies are highlighted throughout this resource, the voice of our community of hero educators remains the critical component to drive and sustain change.

—**Anthony Salcito,** vice president, Microsoft Education
United States

Sail the 7 Cs is a powerful collection of stories, voices, and real-life experiences from educators around the world. The authors provide practical strategies and inspiration and speak to the hearts of all those involved in education. This book is a celebration of educators who have embraced technology and, as a result, have transformed their teaching and learning, innovated, and opened their students' hearts and minds.

—**Iro Stefopoulou,** program lead, Skype in the Classroom
United Kingdom

Becky and Kathi weave together the perfect blend of practical and inspirational as they leverage their own deep experience in addition to that of their educator network. This book is a truly global collaboration and highlights the diversity of educators and stories from every corner of the world. I can't recommend this book enough!

—**Mike Tholfsen,** principal product manager,
Microsoft Education
United States

Sail the 7 Cs provides clear and powerful examples shared by educators to help you create engaging and transformative learning experiences with your students.

—**Gloria Enrique,** postprimary teacher
Ireland

Becky and Kathi will empower you to become a true changemaker in your school through their simple and practical strategies as you and your students brave this exciting sea of communication, collaboration, creation, and many more learning adventures. Bon voyage!

—**Dr. Charlie Miller,** founder and partner
GM of Flipgrid at Microsoft
United States

This book is a most wonderful combination of tools and inspiring stories that will change teachers' practices in classrooms across the world and will influence students' learning processes directly. The authors understand that edtech will never replace the teacher, but when combined with the right pedagogy, it will lead to great outcomes and most certainly a higher grade of engagement.

—**Koen Timmers,** executive director, TAG, inc.; founder of the Kakuma Project, Climate Action Project, and SDG Lab Schools
Belgium

In this book, Becky and Kathi take you on a journey that redefines the Microsoft you might have grown up with and shines a light on the creative potential that teachers and students can achieve with Microsoft tools new and old.

—**Michael Cohen,** speaker, creator, and author
of *Educated by Design*
United States

I loved this book, especially that the content is a collaboration of amazing educators worldwide.

—**Jen Padernal,** educator
Philippines

This interactive book provides a practical guide for classroom teachers and administrators, offering spotlight success stories of global educators in action, creative uses of Microsoft tools and programs, and innovative ready-to-go ideas for classrooms and schools. As practitioners in education themselves, Becky and Kathi speak the language of teachers. This book is a perfect choice for educators looking for inspiration and a deep dive into Microsoft Education and the Microsoft community!

—**Dr. Jennifer Williams,** education activist, professor, and author
United States

Each page offers valuable knowledge and strategies on using digital classroom technologies to empower the educators of today to create the world of tomorrow. Highly recommended if you are a passionate edtech professional, teacher, or student looking for innovative teaching and learning methods.

—**Waqas Shafique,** Microsoft Educator Fellow
Pakistan

Becky and Kathi are at the center of the Microsoft Education community and do a wonderful job of showcasing the value of community and the ways members are using these tools in meaningful and relevant ways.

—**Steve Isaacs,** teacher, game design and development; Minecraft Global Mentor
United States

I loved this comprehensive guide to developing skills with technologies easily within my reach. Reading this felt like having a chat with my coolest, most innovative teacher friends. It's sincere and warm, and it makes teachers like me want to do even better!

—**Nikkie Lange,** associate principal
New Zealand

It has never been more important than now for us to teach our students how to be creative and collaborative communicators. In

Sail the 7 Cs with Microsoft Education, Becky and Kathi provide the playbook to do just that.

—Mike Washburn, director of engagement, Participate;
co-host of *OnEducation Podcast*
United States

Kathi and Becky provide a compass . . . in the form of voices of expert practitioners sharing the way forward through the thoughtful use of technology in support of powerful pedagogies.

—Mark Sparvell, education leader, Microsoft
United States, by way of Australia

Sail the 7 Cs will help you chart a course toward #Onederful learning moments with your students.

—Stephen Eustace, school leader
Ireland

Within the pages of this book, you will explore new possibilities and find the right tools to take you to exciting, new places in your teaching and learning journey! . . . From Collaborators to Creators and all the other Cs in between, this book celebrates a Community of Changemakers and delivers powerful ways to use Microsoft tools in your learning community and beyond.

—Ann Kozma, educator innovation lead, Flipgrid
United States

Grounded in expert knowledge and pedagogy, this book is soon to be a favorite among educators everywhere.

—Shaelynn Farnsworth, educator, learner, and writer
United States

Sail the 7 Cs with Microsoft Education is a must read if you are looking to learn and deploy powerful teaching and learning techniques in your classroom. . . . With firsthand stories and digital resources embedded throughout the book, you will find practical and innovative ideas to provide your students with quality learning experiences and the power of Microsoft.

—Robyn Hrivnatz, program manager, Microsoft US Education
United States

Becky and Kathi have at once combined and amplified the power of the education community by showcasing educators' innovative practices, compassionate outreach to students, and creative use of the powerful tools available in the Microsoft Education toolkit. If you're looking for just one book to inspire educators to transform their students' lives, this is it!

—**Mike Lawrence,** chief maverick, Maverick Learning
United States

Becky and Kathi have brought their unique skill sets and global connections to create a navigational path filled with a treasure trove of educational goodies. . . . Their Anchor Points provide pro tips and big ideas, their Wakelet resources help readers level up, and the embedded Flipgrid QR codes provide the greatest treasure of all: teachers sharing their expertise from all over the globe.

—**Scott Nunes,** ELA teacher turned edtech coach and
cohost of the *TNT Edtech Podcast*
United States

What a ride! The waves of ideas keep on rolling In from cover to cover as Becky and Kathi offer a wealth of experience and inspiration for the classroom. . . . For anyone looking to empower their learners by leveraging tools that are amazingly simple and simply amazing, *Sail the 7 Cs with Microsoft Education* is waiting for you to climb aboard.

—**Michael Drezek,** district technology integrator
United States

SAIL THE 7 Cs
WITH MICROSOFT EDUCATION

SAIL THE 7 Cs
WITH MICROSOFT EDUCATION

Stories from
around the World to
Transform and Inspire
Your Classroom

Becky Keene and Kathi Kersznowski

This book is available at special discounts when purchased in quantity for use educational purposes or as premiums, promotions, or fundraisers. For inquiries and details, contact the publisher at books@daveburgessconsulting.com.

Published by Dave Burgess Consulting, Inc.
San Diego, CA
DaveBurgessConsulting.com

Library of Congress Control Number: 2020935777
Paperback ISBN: 978-1-951600-22-8
Ebook ISBN: 978-1-951600-23-5

Cover and interior design by Liz Schreiter

Contents

INTRODUCTION: WELCOME TO OUR COMMUNITY

As we begin our voyage through the 7 Cs, we need to take a moment to talk about community. It is the Microsoft Education community that introduced the two of us to each other, and it is the Microsoft Education community that has enabled (and inspired) us to write this book. We can't imagine our professional lives without the people, networks, and experiences of the Microsoft Education community.

When we speak of the Microsoft Education community, we are talking about a global community of people from all walks of life who want to embrace the use of the best products, features, and services for teaching and learning. This is a community fully built on the concept of support. We turn to each other to learn new things, get ideas, brainstorm, and find solutions. It is a massive, awesome, interconnected web of people who start off as contacts and very often become friends. Simply by reading this book, you have become a part of our community.

Although this may seem like a book about Microsoft Education tools, it's really a book about promise, people, and pedagogy. It showcases educators from around the world who are using the amazing suite of Microsoft Education tools in genuinely creative and innovative ways. In this book, we celebrate the products and people we see transforming the world of education.

The Promise

If you have never touched or used a Microsoft product in your life, we welcome you! If you're reading this book to just begin exploring Microsoft, we welcome you! If you haven't used Microsoft products in quite some time and wanted to check in to see what's been happening, we welcome you back! And if you're just here to get ideas, you're welcome too! If there's one thing we've learned as we've journeyed deeper into the Microsoft Education community, it's how welcoming it is. Everyone we've met has truly welcomed us with open arms. Often virtually and sometimes in person, we've come together in wide-ranging ways to become more than we could ever be alone. We share, we help, we support, we teach, we listen, we brainstorm, we troubleshoot, we connect, and we become better—together.

The stories we share in this book are not simply a celebration of the magnificent educators who innovate with Microsoft products. Instead, they've been intentionally crafted to model techniques for using these tools that are replicable. Although the narratives and creative ideas of every person spotlighted here are incredible, it was paramount to us that anyone who reads these stories thinks, "Hey, I could do that, too!" More than anything, we want you to feel that familiar mix of imagination, innovation, and craftiness that so often stirs the hearts of teachers when they come across something inspiring.

"Hey, I could do that, too!"

Perhaps most moving is just how much people who are part of the Microsoft Education community love to share. Every single person whose name and story appears in this book emphasized to us how much they benefited from the experiences of others and how they wanted their turn to "pay it forward" by sharing their ideas. We are so very grateful.

The People

As you read through this book, you'll meet people from all over the world. We reached out to our colleagues and connections from six continents to gather stories, anecdotes, and, most of all, examples of how they are transforming education using Microsoft Education tools.

In the pages that follow, you'll see represented a diverse body of educators from more than twenty countries. They are women and men. They teach various subjects and ability levels at primary, secondary, and higher education institutions in rural and urban areas. They are teachers, administrators, librarians, specialists, professors, therapists, activists, and thought leaders. Some are fortunate to have access to quite a bit of technology, while others are working to gain access to even minimal levels.

It is our hope that, as you read these stories, you will find people with whom you can relate, whose stories really resonate, and from whom you can draw inspiration. We are globally connected educators, so selecting who to include was a daunting task. There are hundreds of others we would have liked to have highlighted on these pages. Perhaps there will be sequels in the future, because there are certainly other shining star educators doing brilliant, profound work in education using Microsoft Education tools, and we want you to meet them all.

The Pedagogy

We start with the people, but they are all educators, so pedagogy is their passion. When truly talented educators share their work, it is always about the learning goals and objectives first. This is not a book exclusively about the tools these educators use, but rather an emphatic nod to the ingenuity they employ to make learning relevant. Examples of strong, creative, skillfully constructed pedagogy are woven throughout this book.

We know the Microsoft products we reference are constantly changing and being updated frequently. We are also aware that you may be completely new to Microsoft products, tools, or apps. Perhaps you're even a devout Google-ite or Apple-ian. It's all okay, because this book is about *good teaching*. (And because Office 365 is free for all educators everywhere, you might even decide to try it out.) It's about knowing your learners and making impactful educational opportunities possible for them. It's about crafting lessons that prepare your students for the future. It's about connecting with others to learn best practices for teaching and learning. Hopefully, this book will inspire you to dream big, be brave, try new things, and explore new possibilities in your classrooms and beyond.

Although our focus is on the many diverse uses you can find for the suite of Microsoft Education tools, we have quite consciously not organized the book around the products. There is no OneNote or

Minecraft chapter to follow. Instead, we organized our book around 7 Cs that we have found to be valuable in our own teaching, learning, and professional growth. You may have heard of the 4 Cs, a framework that evolved from the 21st Century Skills movement, which many educators around the world are already familiar with. It stresses that best practices in modern education can be built around four words that start with the letter C: *collaboration*, *communication*, *creativity*, and *critical thinking*.

Hopefully, this book will inspire you to dream big, be brave, try new things, and explore new possibilities in your classrooms and beyond.

But because this is a book about people, you'll find that we included more than these basic four tenets. We have included *community* here in the introduction, because you are now a part of ours, and community has been a core part of our own growth. Our fourth chapter includes two Cs, adding the concept of *computational thinking* to that of critical thinking. They go together as two pieces of the same whole. In fact, some educators note that computational thinking is simply a subset of critical thinking. Finally, we wrap up with a conclusion on becoming *changemakers*. Once you get started using the Microsoft Education tools highlighted herein and adopt the mindset of innovation like so many others have done, we know you will become a changemaker too. We are devoted to encouraging you to be the kind of educators who embody making change in your classroom, your community, and the world.

SAIL THE 7 Cs

- ⚓ Community
- ⚓ Collaborators
- ⚓ Communicators
- ⚓ Creators
- ⚓ Critical Thinkers
- ⚓ Computational Thinkers
- ⚓ Changemakers

The Plan

We truly desire for this book to be an absolute treasure trove of resources. First and foremost, we sought to share stories about the amazing work being done by educators around the world. But we also wanted to include additional material to inspire you.

In each chapter, you will discover instances of us pausing and issuing you a challenge related to the *C* we are investigating in that chapter. These challenges encourage you to ⛵ *Get ready to set sail* and apply what you've read with action. The ideas we suggest are flexible and can be adapted to your students' ages and ability and the subject matter under study. We have no doubt that if you insert these opportunities into your classroom, new things will be learned, and student engagement will be sparked.

At the end of each chapter are anchor points ⚓ . These are big picture takeaways that sum up the key ideas and insights from each chapter. You'll also discover a Crew Member Spotlight: a QR code that links to a Flipgrid video story from one of the educators we want you to meet. You can scan the QR code with any device that has a QR reader, but if you use the Flipgrid app and click the Scan Flipgrid QR button, you'll be able to view that video in augmented reality.

Try it right now! Drop anchor and watch and listen as Emma Nääs from Sweden explains how she builds classroom community with her students.

Have you tried Wakelet? We love Wakelet. It is a curation and organization tool that is the absolute best for the purpose of collecting and distributing links to resources. Although it's not a

Microsoft-created tool, it's definitely a Microsoft Education partner and is well-integrated with Microsoft tools, including Office 365, OneDrive, Teams, Flipgrid, OneNote, and Immersive Reader. You don't need an account to access a Wakelet collection, but you'll probably make one once you see how valuable it is.

To that end, we created a master Wakelet of all the web-based resources and websites mentioned in each chapter. It is broken down into seven C-based Wakelet collections we call "ripples" within our book Wakelet. To access this Wakelet, you can use the link bit.ly/7CsWakelet or simply scan the QR code that follows. You'll want to come back to this collection anytime you see a resource you'd like to access. We've marked the topics that are included in our Wakelet collections with a special Wakelet logo in the margins of this book.

Scan this now!

The Microsoft Education Toolkit

Before we begin, we thought it wise to introduce you to the tools you'll discover in the chapters to follow. We want to take a moment to explain what they are and how they work, so when you encounter them next you can focus on how they are leveraged. What follows is absolutely not meant as a how-to guide to any of these, but rather an orientation to help you grasp what each tool can do so you can understand the amazing ways the educators in this book have put them to use. Feel free to skip this part and come back whenever you need an explanation!

Forms is a Microsoft application that lets users create and distribute digital surveys and assessments. It is a simple yet powerful tool that lets anyone quickly create a Form, collect responses in real time, and view results instantly to visualize the data. Respondents can fill it out on any browser or device. Microsoft Forms gives two generic choices: Forms, which are like surveys, and Quizzes, which allow educators to denote correct answers that can be automatically graded. Teachers have found many ways to use both features to collect feedback, take polls, organize events, measure student knowledge, and assess class progress. When people respond in Forms, the Forms' creator sees real-time data on the Responses tab. Data are presented by student or by question, are represented graphically, and can even be exported to an Excel spreadsheet. The ability to collaborate on the creation of Forms is another feature that educators enjoy. Sharing Forms with students or other recipients can be done by sharing a link, embedding in a webpage, emailing, or even embedding a live Form into a OneNote Class Notebook. One of the most-loved features of Forms in education is the inclusion of Immersive Reader, which gives students the option of having all questions and answer choices read aloud to them.

Flipgrid is for capturing video responses to all kinds of prompts. Flipgrid requires respondents to use devices that have a camera and microphone. Teachers or account owners first create Grids, which are like website communities to which a specified group of students or people are given access. Grid owners then create unlimited Topics within that Grid. Topics are prompts, which are often text-based questions but can also be photos or even videos to which Grid members should respond. Learners create short videos in response to topics. Teachers have many options in regard to personalization and privacy settings, but often a Grid is left "open" so students can see what their peers have recorded. They then have the ability to respond to those videos with videos of their own. Students also now have a variety of integrated tools that allow them to enhance their video responses: screen recordings, filters, drawing tools, emoji, stickers, and whiteboard/blackboard options. The ability for teachers and students to upload videos from other sources allows for "app smashing" with additional educational technology (edtech) tools. Flipgrid allows teachers to build a strong and trusting community of learners, assess students via video responses, and engage students in new ways by allowing them to share their voices. You can create a Flipgrid account at flipgrid.com.

Immersive Reader is the feature available in many Office products and third-party apps that makes text more accessible to all types of readers. It started as a Microsoft Hackathon project as an add-in to OneNote and has expanded since into Word, Outlook, Teams, Flipgrid, Office Lens, Forms, and many more products. Immersive Reader has changed the lives of people around the world, who now have support for reading challenges like dyslexia and dysgraphia, as well as all sorts of verbal, cognitive, neurological, and temporary impairments. Upon launch, Immersive Reader presents a clean space for the reader to manipulate reading options to reduce visual crowding, select a font, label parts of speech, add syllabification, access a picture dictionary, use line view, and even translate by word or entire text at once. Immersive Reader will also read the text aloud to the listener, highlighting words as it goes along, with the correct inflection of the language selected. Because Immersive Reader uses optical character recognition, teachers and students can snap photos of text in books, on posters, and on worksheets and then utilize the viewer to listen to or read the text in more accessible ways.

MakeCode is a block-based coding application accessible on any device through a web browser. Inside MakeCode.com, you will find projects, tutorials, and ideas for students to get started with coding a variety of physical devices, like micro:bit and Circuit Playground (or code in Minecraft as well). Students can also toggle to JavaScript to see the code behind the blocks. MakeCode serves as a great way to introduce students to coding, as well as to expand a student's understanding of computational thinking. Students can design games for each other to play, debug software problems, learn computer science principles, and innovate to change their worlds. Because MakeCode includes an on-screen simulator, a physical device isn't necessary, but if you have one, the projects are more powerful. One of the many reasons we like MakeCode is its ability to integrate with other systems like Adafruit, LEGO, Cue, Arcade, and Chibi Chip.

Minecraft is one of the best-selling video games of all time with over 100 million active monthly users around the world. Microsoft launched an education-specific version that includes assessment tools, a lesson library, and classroom management options, making Minecraft: Education Edition the single most popular game for education because of the limitless possibilities it contains for game-based learning. In creative mode, students have unlimited resources available to build. They can create demonstrations of their learning in any content area, showcasing an understanding of anything from math equations to ancient civilizations. Students can work together to create structures that include electrical components, use code to put their agents to work, and design simple bridges or complicated hydroelectric dams. Educators see engagement increase with this tool and also report students communicating and collaborating on new levels as they work toward a common goal or work peacefully in a common world.

Office Lens is a camera-based application that turns your smartphone or tablet into a powerful portable scanner. This app lets anyone take photographs of a variety of things—documents, whiteboards, worksheets, drawings, receipts, sticky notes, and more—and then enhance those images by cropping, sharpening, brightening, and straightening the photo image. Office Lens can then do many different things with those images. It can convert them to Word documents, PowerPoint files, and PDF files. It can send the scanned document to any OneNote Notebook. It also includes Microsoft's Immersive Reader, which allows it to use optical character recognition to convert an image into readable text and read it aloud right from any device. The result is that a photo of a document or written words becomes a scanned document that is text-based and accessible.

OneDrive is a cloud-based storage platform offered to anyone with a Microsoft account. It's a place to store documents, files, photos, and presentations. When you sign up for a Microsoft account, you're automatically given your own OneDrive account, which is then accessible whenever you sign into your account from any device (yes, there's even an app!). In OneDrive, users can create folders to organize files. They can easily share whole folders or files, and they can prescribe permissions to that sharing (read only or allow editing). OneDrive also has powerful search and filtering features that allow users to quickly and easily find what they need.

OneNote is designed as a holding place for all kinds of content in digital Notebooks. Think of a three-ring binder or planner, with tabs dividing pages into sections. Each OneNote Notebook is its own file, and inside the digital space you can organize notes, images, links, file attachments, lists, audio, drawings, printouts, embedded content, and more. Its organizational structure means that teachers can capture lesson plans, students can capture work, and anyone can keep all sorts of information handy throughout a school year (and beyond). The infinite canvas of each page is a perfect place for brainstorming, sketching, note taking, curating, and list making. Best of all, the search feature looks inside typed text as well as handwritten digital ink and images using optical character recognition. When you store your Notebooks in OneDrive, you can access their contents from any OneNote app or via a web browser from OneNote.com.

Paint 3D is a native app in Windows 10 that brings modeling to life for students. It's easy for students to create objects to reflect their interests, research, or designs—and to render these objects with professional-level tools in a user-friendly interface. With just a few steps, a student can create a 3D object with texture, depth, color, and scale. These objects can be saved and exported to other applications (like PowerPoint) or sent to a 3D printer. Students can also manipulate, repurpose, and remix 3D objects from the in-app library, requiring very little build knowledge yet still allowing students to interact with 3D objects. Combined with digital inking and screen capturing, which are also built into Windows 10 devices, students can narrate their understanding of physical objects in a digital space.

PowerPoint is the ultimate presentation tool. With PowerPoint, teachers and students create stunning and stylized slideshows to engage their audiences. Users can get started by selecting from myriad templates or by creating blank slides and then adding design elements. Anyone can use PowerPoint by simply going to Office. com and creating an account online. Creating an Office account gives users the added convenience of having anything they create automatically saved to their online OneDrive, which means it will be accessible from any device. PowerPoint allows for collaboration, so more than one person can be adding and designing slides. Newer additions to PowerPoint include the Designer, which suggests professional-looking design options for each slide that's created; the ability to add 3D object images to slides; and a Presenter Coach, which uses artificial intelligence to listen to a practice speech and offer helpful suggestions. Another new favorite is the Presentation Translator, which allows attendees to "join" the presentation on their own device, choose from a list of supported languages, and see real-time translation of the presenter's speech on their device.

Sway is a digital storytelling tool that produces high-quality designs for the user. It is available from the Office.com homepage in any web browser. Instead of the user searching for a design that works, Sway will generate designs to match the user's content, including font sets, color schemes, animations, and sizing. One of the best things about Sway is that it is web-based, so it can be used on any device and has a shareable link built in. Because of the built-in design engine, Sway can take a lot less work for students to set up than a traditional PowerPoint. The Remix button is a favorite: Sway uses artificial intelligence to curate colors from the added text. A remix makes a new combination of layout, font, and theme. This is a lot of fun for students and can be "undone" up to ten times back if a certain look appeals after you've seen a few options.

Teams is a one-stop hub for communication and collaboration for a modern teaching and learning environment. Team members can access the resources stored inside the Team, have conversations with one another, join virtual meetings, submit and review assignments (Class Teams), and share files. Channels keep each Team organized by creating subspaces for working on specific projects or units, and Tabs allow for easy-to-access third-party content to sit ready for Team members to view. Want to ask a quick question of a teacher or colleague? Send a chat message. Want to post a question for your entire class to discuss? Start a conversation in your Team. Want to collaborate on a document? Add it to your Files space. Many of the apps you're already using are integrated into Teams, and you'd be surprised how many apps have a Share to Teams button built right in. It's the fastest growing Microsoft tool for good reason: it allows us to have the content, communication, and collaboration we need in one common space accessible from anywhere.

The **Translator** app has narrowed the communication gap for so many families in education systems across the globe. At its simplest, the Microsoft Translator app allows one person to translate spoken, typed, or printed text into another language. More importantly, the Translator app gives one person the ability to speak and translate in real time for another person in the same physical space. It's become so powerful that it's now built right into Word, OneNote, Outlook, and Edge. Even more powerful is the multiuser scenario, allowing someone to launch a conversation from Translate.it to allow anyone to join. Each member of the conversation sees the chat in their language of preference—and hears it, too, if audio is selected.

The **Video Editor** is a simple app with lots of possibilities for education. It is easy to import photos and video into the project library. You can then add content—text, titles, motion, 3D effects, filters, and audio, including tracks from a built-in music library—to the storyboard to edit, split, and trim. Videos can be saved to OneDrive, uploaded to Stream or Flipgrid, or even submitted as a Teams assignment. We love the idea of giving students more options for demonstrating their understanding and showcasing their creativity, and Video Editor does just that. Video Editor can be found by searching for *video* in the Windows 10 search bar, or you can scroll through the apps list to letter *V*.

Whiteboard is a large digital canvas of unlimited space that's made for visual organization and collaboration. Think of it as an infinite, cloud-based whiteboard designed for teamwork and group brainstorming. Whether the rest of your team is in the room, across the school, or across the world, sharing a join link or adding the app to a Teams meeting is all it takes to get everyone in the same planning space. Just sign in with a Microsoft account (or your school Office 365 account) and download the Microsoft Whiteboard app from the Microsoft Store. Everything you create will be accessible from any device, automatically synced, and saved to the cloud. When you use Whiteboard, you'll have the ability to add text or drawings to it using digital ink with a pen, stylus, or touch. You can also use the keyboard to add typed content. Additionally, Whiteboard has several tools that make adding to the canvas even more fun and powerful: you can add sticky notes, change the background color, insert images and PDFs, create tables and charts, and even make handwriting look better. Everything that's added to a Whiteboard can be resized and rearranged by contributors, which makes it the perfect space for group organizing and planning. Whiteboard also includes the Immersive Reader.

Word is the ultimate word publishing tool. It is known throughout the world as the gold standard for creating all kinds of documents. Since 1983, people have been using Microsoft Word to create reports, flyers, pamphlets, résumés, manuscripts, and more. Word gives us rich text editing tools, drawing tools, creative design tools, comprehensive formatting options, and a variety of options for adding images and other decorative elements to any document. Also included are assistive tools like spell checker, a robust dictionary, Immersive Reader, and a powerful translation tool. The online version of Microsoft Word is available at Office.com. Users can access documents from anywhere on any device and let multiple authors contribute to a document via the powerful collaboration feature.

COLLABORATORS

You undoubtedly have read that in the past decade or so, many businesses, organizations, and even schools have shifted their focus from finding highly skilled individuals to seeking potential employees with distinct character traits and abilities. In 2005, former Porsche CEO Peter Schutz was credited with saying, "Hire character, train skill." This philosophy seems to have spread far and wide throughout the world. From Fortune 500 companies to mega-corporations to small businesses, we continue to hear that employers crave applicants with certain qualities. Arguably, first and foremost among them is the ability to collaborate.

There are very few jobs that don't require some degree of collaboration. In fact, most life events hinge on the ability of two or more people to work together. Planning, brainstorming, co-creating, task division, problem solving, and sharing are just some of the ways that people of all ages need to collaborate to maximize efficiency or achieve goals. Much of what we do or want to accomplish in life relies on working together with one or more people. In her book *Reality Is Broken*, Jane McGonigal talks about collaboration as having three parts: cooperating, coordinating, and co-creating. "Collaboration isn't just about achieving a goal or joining forces; it's about creating something together that it would be impossible to create alone." That sounds empowering to us!

Those of us in the field of education depend on the ability to collaborate. We do committees. We have faculty meetings. We are on teams (and now quite literally, Microsoft Teams). We work in departments. We co-teach and co-plan and collaborate all the time. Teaching would be a much harder and surely less appealing job without the support and ideas that we get to share with other educators.

Educators need to prepare students to live and work in an interconnected world. Today's students are already connected through social media, but many have little understanding of *real* project work that includes team productivity and an integration of individual knowledge to create a coherent solution. Unfortunately, quite a lot of collaboration in the classroom today still involves assigning roles to students who work together on a project, having them complete their roles, and then having them combine and submit their work. In many cases, one or two students in the group "lift" the rest of the group to their own higher standards or control the outcome based on their preferences. The students who did less, disagreed, or had limited time and resources are labeled as "slackers" who didn't contribute their fair share, creating frustration and disunity in the group. This model is probably as old as public education itself, and what's truly ironic is that, as a process, it's the opposite of genuine collaboration.

Here's a picture of what we think collaboration really looks like: In the neighborhood Becky lives in, there are five kids who are all around the same age in school. One school year, they decided they wanted to make a movie. They used Word Online through their school Office 365 accounts to collaboratively write a movie script. They worked on it at school during their free time and at home on the weekends. They would initiate live learning experiences by using Skype, having virtual calls back and forth from house to house as questions arose—especially when one family was relocated to Hawaii for a month! They worked together to create a final product (and eventually filmed, edited, and published their movie) using the same methods they see their parents using and that they will be using in their futures. These young learners completed their movie project with no connection to their classrooms. How much more powerful would their education experiences be if these types of collaboration were the norm?

Those of us in the field of education depend on the ability to collaborate.

Because It Takes a Village: Collaborating Using Microsoft Teams

So, what are the right tools to help create authentic collaboration? One of the tools that works to meet all of these components of learning through collaboration is Microsoft Teams. Microsoft Teams has many features that remind users of a learning management system (LMS): assignments, announcements, links to resources, quizzes, and collaborative workspaces. But to call Microsoft Teams a learning management system places artificial boundaries on its uses and limits how one can imagine teachers and students can use Teams to truly collaborate.

Let's start first with how teachers can use Microsoft Teams before illustrating how students can benefit from it. One of the biggest obstacles we've found when a group of educators needs to work together is file sharing. While any of the major industry platforms offer real-time authoring and collaboration (Office Online and G-Suite being the most common), collaborators need a place to store these files that doesn't live on an individual cloud drive. We've all been there: One staff member creates and shares a folder full of resources. Everyone works together on the resources and accesses them in this shared location. Staff member moves or goes on leave, or there is some other life change. Everyone panics because the resources *everyone* accesses are not *everyone's* files. They are *someone's* files. When that person leaves, the files are removed.

Until Staff Teams, that is. Microsoft Teams is built for *anyone's* content to be *everyone's* content, if they are a part of the Team and they keep their shared content in the Teams Files space. People can enter the Team and leave the Team, and the files remain owned by the Team. It is true corporate ownership, and it's so simple that it's beautiful. Even conversations around files are linked to the files themselves, so people are always pointed in the right direction when they need to give feedback, leave comments, make notes, or revise the content.

A quick glance into a Staff Team shows that all members
can post, access content, and share resources.

Recently Becky was working on a shared PowerPoint presentation with a colleague and noticed that he began working on it at the same time. Becky could see his changes happening on his slides while she worked on hers. She had a couple of questions, so she started a quick Chat. When it seemed like they needed to have an actual conversation to get resolution, in one click they were connected via Teams Audio. In five minutes, the two colleagues shared their thoughts, reached a consensus, and made the changes in real time as they talked. An exchange that could have taken several emails over the course of a few days took just a few minutes—all because of the true collaborative nature of the tools available.

Old Bridge Township Public Schools in Old Bridge Township, New Jersey, USA, has undertaken a wide-scale adoption of Microsoft Teams for staff groups, and we got to speak with Jim Yanuzzelli, a technology integration specialist (TIS), about the differences they have seen in the way staff members collaborate since they implemented Teams. One example he provided is that Old Bridge Township school district's TISs have found that the Meet Now component allows teachers to quickly get resolution to time-sink issues that would have normally derailed a lesson. Now, when a teacher distributes a Form and the students can't access it, the teacher can pop over to Teams for a Meet Now chat with Jim or one of his colleagues. Teachers in any location in the district can quickly call the TIS team over Teams, share their screen, and get help. This allows Jim and his colleagues to support teachers in real-time situations and makes the TIS crew a collaborative part of the success of the classroom lesson.

Meet Now is easy to overlook. Select the video icon
in Teams in the conversation box to get started.

Each building in Old Bridge has set up a Team for their staff professional learning communities, which has allowed them to transition to meet virtually for 50 percent of their team meetings. Though prevalent in the modern business world, the idea that teachers can join from anywhere and can collaborate productively without sharing a physical space is revolutionary in the education industry. In Old Bridge, school administrators leave assignments for the staff members to complete outside of their face-to-face meetings, including journal article readings that require a response. This allows teachers to think and communicate thoughtful responses to critical issues without being put on the spot to share in a whole group setting.

Indeed, one of the most important insights that Jim and his colleagues have had is that everyone on a Team has a bit of knowledge and expertise to share that makes everyone in the group better. Educators who are new to the field, quiet in large group meetings, or absent due to personal issues can still contribute to the Team and therefore be recognized for adding value. The collaborative components in Teams have brought a fresh culture of inclusion and awareness of others' strengths to the participants, and that can only be a good thing.

Each content department and class in Old Bridge also has a Team. Departments and classes can share rubrics, handouts, and other team-wide resources to be accessed by anyone who needs them. They also use the conversation space to send alerts and information without having to churn through email. Class Teams are perfect for managing workflow with the assignments, grading, quizzes, and other tools built right in (multiple choice quizzes can even be autograded!). Teachers arrange their Teams interface to include tabs across the top for their most current and relevant content and integrate OneNote Class Notebook (described in depth in another chapter) right inside. Students benefit because all the materials for their **W** classes exists in a single repository.

All of these options have allowed teachers to "rethink the teaching and learning assessment cycle," according to Scott Bricker, Director of Educational Technology at Santa Margarita Catholic High School in Rancho Santa Margarita, California, USA. One of his precalculus teachers told him about receiving a Chat direct message from a student who had a question. He popped into the student's private section in the OneNote Class Notebook via Microsoft Teams and left ink and audio feedback on the student's work. Another great example of how teachers are changing their approach is how they hold office hours. The teacher hosts test review sessions the afternoon before an exam, and students can join and watch as their teacher shares his or her desktop to work through questions or problems for which kids have requested help.

Scott also has a group of students who were accepted to present at an out-of-state conference about the way they've used Teams for their Model United Nations project. The students approached the staff advisors for their class and asked to use Teams to organize their work, claiming it would help with productivity and efficiency as well as the goal of improved collaboration and communication. With searchable content and the ability to work from anywhere, these students are now using business-class tools to complete tasks and work in a shared responsibility space.

Scott's educators have long been concerned about how to work together with families to support students in need—ones who have been out for physical or mental health concerns and who have missed a significant section of their school life. Often these students can join one or two classes remotely via Microsoft Teams video call or at least hold a virtual check-in meeting with their teacher when they aren't able to come to campus. "Students and families in these stressful situations don't need 'one more thing,'" Scott explained to us. "They need for us to reduce their stress and meet them where they are."

Passing Notes in Class: Collaborating Using OneNote

When Becky taught middle-school Humanities (ages eleven to fourteen), students were so used to collaborating in shared OneNote Notebooks that it was the first action they would take at the start of a new group project. "Who's making the Notebook?" could be heard all around the room during the initial work session. Students knew they couldn't work together without a shared space, and the collaborative nature of OneNote, combined with its flexible content-rich pages, was perfect for brainstorming, list making, sketching, and designing.

During a simulation teaching her students about ancient Mesopotamia, Becky broke her students into teams she called tribes. Each tribe worked on projects showing their knowledge of the ancient culture, earning points toward purchasing resources for their tribe, like building materials, weapons, and food. Much like in a game of Risk, students had a daily opportunity to move their tribe around the map and conquer lands with their points. Students worked together at school to complete tasks, but they also worked together from home. Because OneNote works offline, students who didn't have internet access away from school (but who did have devices) spent time writing, reading, and editing work in the shared Notebook. Upon return to school the next day, their work synced into the Notebook for other students to view. Each student could contribute to the tribe—and its success—because of this increased access.

The familiarity of students with OneNote makes us want to share this remarkable story about collaboration from Melanie LeJeune, who is a technology coach/librarian at St. Louis Catholic High School in Lake Charles, Louisiana, USA.

> I was doing a student training at the beginning of the school year, and I wore my OneNote cape. On Twitter, you're always seeing things about "OneNote Avengers." One of the students said, "Can I get a cape?" and I said, "Well, you have to earn it." I knew he was a kid who was really interested in technology, so I said, "Let me figure out how you're going to earn it, and I'll get back to you."
>
> I got together with our teachers and asked what kind of skills they thought a OneNote Student Avenger should possess, and they helped me to formulate a list. We already have a Computer

Architecture class, and those are the students who learn how to repair our computers (we are a 1:1 school), so we started with them and got all of them to "test" to become a Student Avenger. They had to demonstrate that they could do those skills we had decided were needed for an Avenger. Once they did that, they earned their cape and took an oath.

The idea is that they are our first line of defense. If they are in a classroom and a teacher or student has an issue, then they can offer their services. These students don't get called out of class to help others, but they can help someone if issues arise in their own classroom. We keep our Avenger list on our learning management system, so all of the teachers know who the Avengers in the school are. I advertise that list in our school newsletter, too, so everyone is aware of who the Student Avengers are.

I created a OneNote Class Notebook for these Avengers, and in that Notebook they keep track of their work logs. They record the issues they encounter. I'm able to see each issue in our shared Notebook because the section or page turns bold, and if they did resolve it, I usually give them a sticker or something on that page. We also use the Notebook's collaboration space to keep instructions that come up for how to tackle different issues. It's great when the student takes the lead. I have Avengers who figure out how to solve the problems and then put the instructions in the Notebook for everyone else.

The story of the Student Avengers is one that you can replicate in your own school system. It not only offers a much-needed service to teachers, but models what genuine collaboration looks like for students. **W**

There is no doubt that OneNote is a valuable collaborative tool for teachers and students, but we've found that it is important to keep in mind that other education professionals in our school systems can benefit from using OneNote as well. In Kathi's role as a technology integration specialist, she frequently offers workshops and professional development to teachers. She admittedly hadn't thought to involve therapists and other specialists in her workshops, but one day occupational therapist Jill McGinley-Brett approached her and mentioned that she had been hearing wonderful things about OneNote. After learning about OneNote from Kathi, Jill immediately saw the value in setting up a OneNote Notebook for her therapy logs. She was then able to share that document with other school professionals who provide services to the same children. She keeps fastidious notes of each session because it is so easy to do so. The other specialists can share a page, see Jill's progress notes with each child, and add their own notes so that the entire service team is able to deliver coordinated service plans without having meetings. Jill's story is a reminder to all of us to remember to include everyone in our buildings who can benefit from the Microsoft tools. Many of our colleagues often have unique needs and ways to get good use out of these programs, especially when it comes to collaborating with each other—and there is usually a Jill in the group who is the perfect person to get others excited about the possibilities of Microsoft's collaboration tools . . . and dream up some new ones!

Here's a peek into a OneNote Notebook shared among educators. Notice the section tabs on the left, the pages inside the section in the second column from the left, and the page content in the middle. On the right is the Share pane, and you can see lots of educators are using this Notebook together.

From Russia with Love: Collaborating Using Flipgrid

One of the simplest definitions of collaboration is *working together to produce something*. In many of these examples that follow, students aren't creating large projects, research papers, or presentations. Instead, the product in some of our stories is experiences. These experiences resonate with students forever, because they have connected with someone else in another place. They have jointly created an opportunity for collaboration, learning, and engagement that would have never happened otherwise. Sometimes the "something" that has been produced isn't tangible—but it is unmistakable.

One of the teachers we have gotten to know through the Microsoft community is Anna Dyagileva. Anna lives in Yamalo-Nenets Autonomous Okrug, Labytnangi, Russia. She teaches students ranging in age from eight to seventeen and is the head of the English Club Community. Anna is a Flipgrid Global Student Voice Ambassador, and she uses Flipgrid to collaborate with other Russian educators, and she even has her students collaborating with other students through Flipgrid's GridPals feature.

She began her Flipgrid journey like most of us—sharing simple prompts and allowing her students to express themselves informally. Anna told them it was a form of blogging, and this built their confidence in sharing their voices. She asked them to answer longer prompts in English and to practice their vocabulary. One way they do this is through storytelling with #Flipmoji scenes, which involve students using emoji within Flipgrid. The students then appear and speak as a main character in that scene. The students love collaborating to create, compare, and share stories in English. Even Anna's shy students became more confident with their English by using Flipgrid's filters and emoji.

After a while, Anna's students asked for more and more Flipgrid prompts and opportunities to speak, so she created a project for them. Anna had her students do research about Russia, finding facts and even pictures that they could share to a Grid. To make the project carry much more meaning for her students, Anna decided to share those facts and that Grid with the world. Did this make her students practice their English with more determination and precision? Absolutely! Did this increase the quality of the facts they gathered because they were proud to share about their country with others around the world? You bet! They started to use and explore the other features in Flipgrid, writing text captions on their video and even adding pictures as stickers that appeared as they spoke. Anna says that the students took tremendous pride in this project because of its worldwide reach, and they really felt the impact of knowing that others were listening to them.

They really felt the impact of knowing that others were listening to them.

Flipgrid offers several collaborative opportunities. Anna has added seven other "copilots" (educators who are co-administrators) from Russia to her Grids. She's literally connecting other Russian educators to her project, expanding its reach and giving a bigger platform to more students who are eager to be heard. Teachers like Anna, who allow students to collaborate through Flipgrid, sometimes find themselves giving voices to those who were voiceless.

One of the remarkable collaboration features of Flipgrid is GridPals, which allows users to find others who are interested in collaborating. In 2017, a Flipgrid Ambassador named Bonnie McClelland from Long Island, New York, USA, came up with this idea. She knew that these students who were blossoming into passionate, empathetic, brave speakers felt valued and validated when others heard what they had to say. She saw how students craved feedback from their peers and other people besides their teacher. Bonnie wanted to give those students a way to connect with other classrooms. For a while, Bonnie was manually matching people who were interested, but, of course, soon everyone wanted this feature, so the team at Flipgrid jumped in to help. In summer 2018, they announced that Flipgrid had built Bonnie's idea right into the platform! Bonnie's idea had become such a phenomenon that it's now an indelible part of the Flipgrid website.

We asked Bonnie to tell us a little about how she felt about the development of GridPals and its international success as a platform to connect student voices from around the world.

I cannot be more thrilled to see Flipgrid GridPals interacting and learning with each other all over the globe! My vision was to have a platform so that students everywhere could connect, have virtual buddies, and appreciate cultures and the world outside of their classrooms. Flipgrid was the perfect tool! Time zones and postage were no longer an issue. Students recorded videos and woke up the next morning to replies! The reactions I've seen when kids make a special connection with a peer in another area of the world is simply priceless. As educators, we want what's best for our students. Flattening our classroom walls and collaborating with fellow teachers to create these unforgettable learning experiences has truly been a journey that keeps getting better. I cannot wait to see what the future of GridPals holds!

Get ready to set sail: Log in to the Educator Dashboard at flipgrid.com, then select #GridPals from the top of the page. Set up your profile, and connect with one educator.

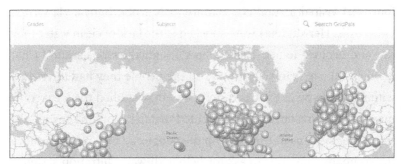

Find your GridPal by visiting Flipgrid.com and connecting with one of thousands of other teachers in the world!

The First Rule of Skype Club: Collaborating Using Skype in the Classroom

In 2015, a Belgian educator named Koen Timmers started a project to help students in Kakuma, Kenya receive instruction via Skype. He recruited other teachers to join him, and soon a small group of dedicated educators from around the world was providing live instruction to kids desperate to learn half a world away. Now Koen has a collaboration with Dr. Jane Goodall called Innovation Lab Schools in which they aim to offer free, quality education to one million African children utilizing more than one thousand teachers across ninety countries—all delivered through virtual calls using Skype!

Another moving example of the power of Skype in the Classroom to change the world comes from Stacey Ryan and her teammates Dyane Smokorowski and Andrea Friend. They found each other via the Skype in the Classroom community and then connected virtually. Stacey was a middle school math teacher (and is now a tech coach) in Wichita, Kansas, USA, where her students (ages eleven to fourteen) visited a rural community in Nairobi, Kenya, via virtual video calls. Her students were shocked at the lack of clean water they saw and decided to act. The students designed lessons around what it would take to bring clean water to the people they had interacted with using Skype in the Classroom, and they studied the local community and its resources. They decided that they couldn't design and ship water systems in time to help the people, so they reached out to the company LifeStraw to ask for help with water filtration systems. The team member at LifeStraw helped them understand what it would take to fundraise for a new system; they also agreed to match their contributions.

Stacey's class quickly got the whole school to start fundraising. Coin drives, donations, and awareness campaigns became the students' focus outside of their academics. One can only image the amount of writing and communication involved with their actions and the math involved with calculating cost and contributions over and over. Finally, the students reached their goal and raised enough money for new water systems for a community an entire world away. Thanks to video calls made possible by Skype in the Classroom, they got to see the fruits of their labor as the people celebrated with their fresh drinking and handwashing water.

Stacey, Dyane, and their students literally changed the lives of people on the other side of the world. Stories like these both warm our hearts and spark our motivation to achieve even greater heights of collaboration.

One of the greatest examples of creativity in collaboration comes from a world-class educator from Wales named Paul "Lanny" Watkins. Lanny is a true innovator who has a talent for thinking of the big picture and often outside the box when it comes to his students. Lanny is a teacher of Information and Communication Technology (ICT) and computing at Ysgol Bae Baglan, a Microsoft Showcase School in North Port Talbot, Wales. He has an inspiring tale to share about how he invented something called Skype Club. We are pretty sure that most of our readers have used video calling before, but this takes it to an entirely new level. Building learning experiences using Skype in the Classroom requires working together—and it produces something especially memorable for students.

> One day, our headmaster happened to say, "I need the list of field trips that we're going to run as rewards." Some of these were to theme parks or to go to the beach for surfing. I said, "I want to run a Skype Day. I want to take the kids around the world." I

had thirty-five kids that signed on to do my trip. They came into school at eight in the morning, and we had everyone pack as if they were going on a trip, so they brought in a packed lunch with them and everything. From eight in the morning until seven in the evening, we just did Skype calls around the world. We were Skyping with ordinary people, influential people. We did virtual field trips. We had directors of Microsoft and product people.

One minute we were in New York, and the next minute we were in Cape Town, and then in Brazil, and then we were in Greece, and then we went to London . . . Later in the day, students came back from the other field trips saying that they had just been to the beach, but these Skype Club kids said, "Well, we've been to New York and South Africa and . . ." The kids were on overload!

Originally, our school didn't have access to Skype, so I had to ask our district for special permission. Then, I invited the heads of IT from our district to be at our school for one of the calls. They came and, after watching for an hour, said, "We're going to open Skype up to every single school in our district. We've never seen anything like it, and all schools need to have access to this. We actually saw the children growing in front of us." Skype was used for the experience but also to get the people who have the power to throw the switch . . . and it worked!

The school I was in wanted to start a pupil enrichment program, and part of my job is also training the staff, so I thought I'd kill two birds with one stone. I decided to set up a Skype Club using the field trip as the idea. There was no time to go in and train teachers on how to use Skype in their subject areas, so I literally would have Wednesday lunch times where we would play Mystery Skype, and then Wednesday after school we would do a virtual field trip. I'd invite the teachers to come in and participate the same way the kids are. I said, "You don't need to be there to do any of the classroom management. You don't have to prepare a thing. Just come in." As a result of that, teachers were coming in, and they'd say, "Can I do this in my lessons?" And I said, "Yeah, let's sit down, and we'll talk about it."

It opened doors up for me to work with departments because it wasn't some person just saying, "Oh, I've heard you talk about using Skype in the Classroom in your lessons." They actually experienced it. I didn't have to do one more thing. That was it. They were hooked.

The head of geography actually took me aside and said, "I'm such a control freak. I don't like people coming into my classroom and teaching my kids because I know how they need to be taught." He is an excellent teacher. So, I sat down with him and asked, "What are you teaching the kids at the moment?" He said, "Oh, we're doing map reading." I said, "Well, have you ever thought about having an explorer teach the children how to read a map?" I continued, "Look, I'll be there. I'll set up the camera. It's just like introducing a live guest speaker who might come into your classroom." He admitted to me later that it began as the most nerve-wracking hour of his life because he was worried that something was going to go wrong. At the end of the lesson, I asked him how he felt about it, and he said, "I've been teaching for eighteen years, and that was the highlight of my teaching career."

Lanny concluded our interview by stressing the fact that his idea is completely replicable. You can start this movement at your school. Sometimes it just takes one person with one idea to light a spark that will catch fire and create a brighter future for the students we serve—and then one other person, on the other end of the Skype in the Classroom virtual call, willing to collaborate on building new types of learning experiences for students.

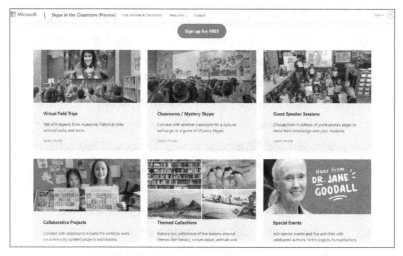

The Skype in the Classroom website is full of amazing ideas and opportunities to use with your students.

Steve Auslander teaches at Allisonville Elementary School in Indianapolis, Indiana, USA. He is a Skype Master Teacher and an enthusiast for connecting via the Skype in the Classroom community. Through this community, Steve has met people from all over the world, and many of these people have become his friends. As Steve's friendships have grown, so have his collaborative ideas. Being global friends with other teachers who are "tech-venturous" has many benefits, including a pervasive feeling of "Why not? Let's try it!"

Being global friends with other teachers who are "tech-venturous" has many benefits

That's exactly what happened when Steve collaborated with two of his Skype in the Classroom buddies to see if they could run a web-based quiz game called Kahoot right through virtual calls by tapping into their familiarity with Skype in the Classroom. They soon had hundreds and hundreds of kids collaborating from countries all over the world. Here's how Skype Kahoot got started and how you can join in the fun.

The whole thing started with my friends Lanny Watkins from Wales and Steve Sherman from South Africa. I teach a two-week science and technology summer camp for my district. One thing that my principal let me do was plan a Kahoot, and I decided that since it was the summer, I was just going to make it fun. The three of us created a fun pop culture Kahoot game for all of our students. We were able to make it work with the time zones. It was first thing in the morning in Indiana, it was two in the afternoon in Wales, and it was maybe half past three in the afternoon in South Africa. The kids loved it, and they were singing along to all the different songs we included that were popular at the time. At the very end, there was a "floss-off"—that crazy dance thing that all the kids seem to know in every part of the world? They were all flossing! It was hysterical!

Lanny realized that this was a big idea, that this could be really big. At first, I thought, *No, this is just fun.*

But we kept talking about it, and we decided that we were going to amp it up a little bit for the annual Microsoft event known as Skype-a-Thon (now known as Microsoft Global Learning Connection) in 2017. We had a ten-country Kahoot over Skype using screen sharing. It was Mexico, Malaysia, South Africa, Wales, Nigeria . . . ten countries in all. It was a lot of fun, and we all had the goal of teaching kids that it doesn't matter where you live, everybody knows that Shrek lives in a swamp, everybody knows Taylor Swift's lyrics. . . . We are more alike than we are different, and that was the message.

Lanny and Steve kept saying, "We've got to make this bigger," and so we did. The next year we were able to get thirty countries involved with four different time slots! We even had one for the Far East, so on Monday night in Indiana, which was Tuesday morning there, we facilitated a Kahoot that involved China, Vietnam, Sri Lanka, Russia, and other countries. There were over seventy participating classrooms and hundreds and hundreds of kids! It was such a blast! Questions ranged from sports to music to cinema . . . all these different categories that showed just how much we all love the same things.

The whole Kahoot experience was one of my favorite moments of all time. The kids were singing along, everyone was waving their flags, and at the very end everyone was dancing together. It was great!

Steve points out that his Skype Kahoot idea could be used for any collaboration any time and could be based on any lesson objectives. For instance, if your class is learning in math about the order of operations, you could organize a Kahoot with one or more classes, and your students will see that this lesson is relevant in other places too. Try creating one around a book study or gamify some collaborative knowledge about a current event or global issue. When students around the world are playing the same game at the same time, it shows them that what they are learning is meaningful and relevant.

Get ready to set sail: Visit the Skype in the Classroom community at skypeintheclassroom.com to schedule your calls with classrooms and experts from around the world or take virtual field trips to museums, zoos, parks, and more amazing places.

Not Just Playing Games:
Collaborating Using Minecraft

One of the top things we think about when we hear the word *Minecraft* is that students are playing games . . . together. Becky has two Minecraft-playing children at her house, but when they play Minecraft, there are usually even more children involved. Sometimes six kids are all crafting together in her living room— learning together, talking to each other, asking for help, sharing resources, and problem solving as they work. It's quite amazing to listen in on their conversations and realize the amount of interdependence involved. Search YouTube for Minecraft, and you'll find thousands of tutorial videos and amazing builds, but you'll also find that group projects abound. Students, teens, young adults, and adults are all working in teams to survive, create, and play.

Becky recently taught a literacy lesson to a group of fourth- and fifth-grade students (ages ten to eleven). She talked about how the basic elements of literature, like plot and setting, impact a story. The students were tasked with creating a scene from a recent novel in Minecraft: Education Edition, one in which the setting was extremely important. Many students opted to work in groups, and it was remarkable to watch them lean in, heads together, sketching and talking and planning. They reviewed materials available in Minecraft, discussed what components of the setting were most important to include, and decided together how these components could be built. They also shared responsibility, making plans about who would create the world, who would build what, and where to begin. As they worked over the course of a few weeks of computer lab time, Becky heard lots of collaboration happening. They encouraged one another to work, to move forward, and to contribute. They had ownership in the process, and they were so proud of the work they'd completed when finished. She and the librarian at the school invited younger students into the computer lab one day to tour the scenes and hear about the stories the older students had read . . . and then they escorted them next door to the library to check out some new recommended books.

Students working on planning pages and Minecraft builds for the story setting activity.

We had the opportunity to speak with Amanda Calitz, a faculty lecturer at the University of the Witwatersrand in Johannesburg, South Africa, about how her higher-education students are using Minecraft for their own collaborative learning experiences. These nursing students are pursuing their health science education degrees and have a wide range of ages and experience among them. Amanda told us about a health system project they completed recently that asked students to explain a human body system by building a working model in Minecraft. While her students worked on their own projects, they also supported each other in collaborative ways. Amanda noticed, for example, that they seemed to pair up naturally so that nurses with a richer expertise in nursing pedagogies and practice were working alongside nurses who felt more comfortable with the digital skills required to complete the project. An oncology nurse created a model of a human breast with red blocks placed where the markers should be and blue blocks where the cancer may spread first. Another nurse created a model of the stomach in which the player ventured into the stomach itself and was greeted by signage explaining the different parts of the digestive process. The nurse included blocks of lava inside the stomach in the game, which simulated the acid in the stomach lining, and then signage on how to administer "an antacid" by breaking glass to release water into the stomach (the water in the game helps extinguish the lava much like an antacid would contain burning sensations in a real stomach). Amanda noted that these "individual" projects were highly collaborative exercises because everyone noticed how they needed each other to make their projects the best they could be. When students help each other to make their individual work better, it builds a classroom culture any educator can be proud of.

 Get ready to set sail: Brainstorm ways students could be demonstrating their understanding of concepts in your curriculum in Minecraft: Education Edition. If you haven't already, download it from aka.ms/download and use your Office 365 for Education account to try it out.

Nelly Hamed, a Microsoft Innovative Educator Expert at Hayah International Academy in Cairo, Egypt, attended the Microsoft Global Educator Forum (now called E2) in Redmond, Washington, USA, in 2015. She is now responsible for transforming the lives of teachers in her country—and thus the students as well. Her story illustrates the power of becoming part of the collaborative Microsoft community.

My story is not with one class of students; it's about the teachers in my country, who then can reach thousands and thousands of students. When I participated in E2 for the first time, it changed my way of thinking and teaching in my class. After I returned home, I decided to deliver all that I had learned to teachers all over my country. Collaborating with Microsoft Egypt and the Ministry of Education, I started to lead completely free trainings for teachers to increase the awareness of the importance of using technology in education. I found Minecraft: Education Edition is brilliant because it teaches students how to think and how to solve problems. I started to do online sessions and even face-to-face trainings about Minecraft in education. The teachers started using Minecraft in their classes and in their projects—and some of them are even earning their master's degrees and PhDs in how they can use Minecraft in teaching and learning. Today I am so proud to see a lot of teachers in Egypt have an impact in every field.

But perhaps the most powerful story we've encountered regarding collaboration and Minecraft involves student agency. It's a fairly new term in education that means that students choose to act with purpose to produce a particular result, often on behalf of a service, person, or group. What's fun about agency is that it can take a student anywhere, and teachers can guide the empowerment to a greater good. It can be on a small scale or wide-reaching, and it can be prescriptive or open-ended. It can even wind up directed at helping teachers!

Atlanta Public Schools in Atlanta, Georgia, USA, has a diverse population of students. It is a mostly urban area, with a digital divide among students who have access to resources at home and those who do not. Felisa Ford, a digital learning specialist for Atlanta Public Schools, is a champion of student agency. She spent some time talking with us about the Minecraft Student Ambassador program she helps run in the middle schools she supports.

When Atlanta's six thousand middle-school students (ages eleven to fourteen) began to receive 1:1 devices, the students were thrilled. Teachers began providing more robust lessons because the students had access to devices at home, and student-to-student collaboration increased beyond the school day. Yet, while students were extremely excited to see Minecraft: Education Edition available on their new Lenovo 300s, teachers weren't quite ready to build lessons around Minecraft in the classroom.

Felisa told us how they focused at first on training teachers. They found that, while teachers were interested in Minecraft and attended trainings with excitement, they weren't really diving into using Minecraft with students at the level of adoption the digital learning team hoped for. So, Felisa and her team developed a new approach: let the students be the champions. What if teachers don't have to be the experts? What if teachers just *allowed* students to use Minecraft to demonstrate their knowledge and understanding of content, to submit a world build for a choice project, or to work together to complete a shared task?

Let the students be the champions.

They also created a student Minecraft Ambassador Program. Students were taught how to deliver a Minecraft training—to both students and teachers—and were provided with scripts and educational examples to share, many of which they helped brainstorm along the way. The students prepared lessons and challenges that could be used by middle-school teachers in their own classrooms, and they made sure they understood the teachers' concerns about classroom management so they could speak to those things as well.

"This is our version of a flipped professional development," Felisa explained to us, "in which the students are the advocates!" This model also allowed the students to demonstrate mastery in Minecraft in front of an audience and gave them opportunities to collaborate as they showed what they were able to do in a completely different framework.

The Minecraft Student Ambassadors of Atlanta Public Schools are authentic collaborators. They show teachers what it means to use Minecraft in the classroom, teach students how to use it appropriately, and open new learning pathways for both. Ambassadors recently presented at a local edcamp and then at a statewide education technology conference, and they often set up a table at district-wide events to spread awareness about their program. Felisa and her team are rightly proud of this group and the way they have given agency to these students to make a difference: "These students have been an essential part of our growth, and we wouldn't be in the place we are without them." That's the power of collaboration in a nutshell.

Conclusion

At this point, it will not come as a surprise to discover that this book was entirely written using Microsoft tools to collaborate. Becky lives near Seattle, Washington, and Kathi lives in southern New Jersey. We are almost three thousand miles apart from one another, but we feel as close as can be thanks to all the tools we used to stay in touch, brainstorm, share resources, ask each other questions, and literally write this entire book. We did not meet in person once—we just didn't need to. We had virtual calls in Teams once every week or so. We are copilots of a Flipgrid in which we collected some of our interviews.

We had our ideas and chapters in a shared OneNote Notebook, and we drafted our entire book using sections and tabs. For example, we had a page with a table that we used to keep track of whom we were interviewing and about which topics. Each person we interviewed had his/her own page in our Interviews section. Kathi even used the audio recording feature to record several of her interviews, and then used the dictation feature to write whole sections when she was feeling inspired but didn't feel like typing. In OneNote, we could each see what the other had written, we could ask and answer each other's questions, and we even kept meeting notes. When we were ready, we pulled our writing out of the OneNote Notebook sections and put each collaborative chapter into shared Word documents that we kept in a shared OneDrive.

The ability to use Microsoft Education tools to communicate with people across the country and around the world never ceases to amaze us. Our final story is about one educator who uses Microsoft Education tools on Twitter to communicate with other teachers about Microsoft Education tools. Marjolein Hoekstra from The Hague, South Holland, Netherlands is one of those people whose Twitter handles—@MSEduCentral and @TweetMeet—are instantly recognizable in the Microsoft Education community. She runs one of the largest and most popular Twitter chats in the world. A Twitter chat is an pre-advertised event that's held on Twitter in which a bunch of people from anywhere in the world participate simply by using a designated hashtag to find and reply to conversations. Marjolein and her teammates Francisco Texeira and Anica Trickovic have created the hashtag #MSFTEduChat to have themed online discussions every single month. For each discussion, they scour the Microsoft Education community for experts and enthusiasts about the topic of the month, and Marjolein spends a great deal of time welcoming them and using Microsoft Education tools to prepare them to be the hosts for the global chat. Marjolein explains:

Every month we use Microsoft OneNote and Teams to guide the hosts of the global and multilingual #MSFTEduChat TweetMeets through a training program that prepares these hosts for event day. We offer the hosts our Twitter Timeline Spreadsheet to help them promote the event to their followers and schedule tweets about the discussion questions for event time.

With Flipgrid, the hosts learn how to prepare their own video script and record their video. They're invited to talk about the topic of that month's TweetMeet, their experiences with students, and stories that excite them. TweetMeet Fans can use our PowerPoint template to create their own TweetMeet Friend Card. These cards, which show that person's picture and a short text about their passion for the upcoming TweetMeet topic, have become quite popular.

Since the two of us have both been global TweetMeet hosts in the past, we can tell you that it was not just an honor and an education to be part of that group of hosts. Marjolein coordinates a virtual video chat, so the hosts can all get to know each other first. It is pretty exhilarating to be on a video chat with people from so many countries and listen to them share some things about themselves. Then, as hosts, we collaboratively worked together to plan an international Twitter chat. Marjolein had a highly detailed, brilliantly organized OneNote Notebook with spreadsheets, timelines, tips, PowerPoints, and links to tutorials. She even taught many of the hosts how to use Flipgrid so that everyone could upload videos. She was our teacher, our organizer, and soon became our friend.

We would love to have our readers get involved. Just follow the hashtag, join the chats monthly, and when you're ready, reach out to Marjolein. Her #MSFTEduChat TweetMeets have grown even larger, and now not only does she use Teams, but she also has a great team that helps her get this organized and translated into multiple languages.

Get ready to set sail: Visit twitter.com/tweetmeet from your favorite browser. Check the schedule (usually the banner image) for the next TweetMeet, then mark your calendar to join in. If you're new to Twitter, you can also be a lurker. Just check back on that same link during the chat time and watch the great ideas flood in.

Go follow or view the @TweetMeet handle on Twitter if you're interested in learning and connecting with other educators.

We're not sure which of the ideas above excites us more: educators saving time as professionals because they have the right tools and environments to support their work, kids building shared products, or students learning alongside others or working together to produce meaningful experiences. We covered a lot in this chapter! Think about which idea resonated most with you. Which one solved a problem, ignited your curiosity, or renewed your energy for trying something new? Start there—then invite a colleague to join you. But beware of where it will lead you—an invitation might result in a book of your own!

Collaboration Anchor Points

⚓ Give students opportunities to collaborate that emulate what they will need to do to work productively with others after they leave your education system.

⚓ Choose tools that allow for the best collaborative practices with the least amount of challenges.

⚓ Reach out to other teachers to co-produce authentic collaborative experiences kids will never forget.

Crew Member Spotlight:
Lanny Watkins

Paul 'Lanny' Watkins

Watch and listen as Lanny Watkins from Wales shares his message on the importance of collaboration.

Use your Flipgrid app to scan the QR code for an augmented reality experience or use any QR code reader to view as a standard video. You can also access the link to this video from the Wakelet collection for this chapter.

COMMUNICATORS

Kathi remembers sitting in her very first graduate course in educational leadership for her school administration degree. There were twelve educators in the cohort who hoped to become school leaders—principals, directors, supervisors, or even superintendents. One of the very first activities the professor did was ask each student to generate a list of ten qualities they felt were most important for leaders. They were given time to generate lists privately, and then they were asked to share with the class and compare results.

As the professor posted answers on the board, he began using tally marks to indicate repeated answers. In the end, the responses from twelve very different educators from twelve very different educational settings had some very surprising similarities. What Kathi remembers most about this activity is the answer that every single student had given: communication.

Think back to a time when you felt underinformed (or not informed at all). Perhaps you didn't know how to complete a project, you didn't submit something on time, you missed details that made you feel foolish, or you even felt hurt that others seemingly knew things that you hadn't been told. You probably felt out of the loop. You may have felt lost, and you most certainly felt confused. Communication breakdowns can cause a multitude of problems.

As educators whose very job it is to spend every day conveying messages and learning, we know the importance of perpetually communicating. As a collective group, we probably believe in over-communicating for the sake of making sure everyone feels informed. Students, teachers, families, and even school leaders like to feel they are well informed about what is expected and what's happening in their world.

But even more to the point is the fact that communication is the very backbone of education. Those of us in education rely on every aspect of communication: expressive, receptive, verbal, nonverbal, written, spoken, gestural, symbolic. We know that when any factor or nuance of the communication process is hindered, the desired result is derailed. Much of the time, the desired result is simply comprehension. Teachers are doing everything they can to promote understanding: of content, of each other, and of the world. Without understanding, we're not really educating. Our job is to communicate content and to do it effectively. We must model these skills for our students, who in turn need to communicate their knowledge of content to and interact with a range of audiences.

So, we, like most of you, seek ways to get creative in our communication. We want to reach the most people in a wide variety of ways. Some folks appreciate brevity. Others crave details inside of details inside of details. Many educators want collaborative communication that includes ways for all members to contribute and feel valued. Some students won't even glance at something unless there's a hook—brightly colored graphics, a video, a meme, or even the promise of a prize.

The Microsoft Education toolkit offers so many tools to make communication in our educational settings not only effective but also fun. As champions of communication, you can use Microsoft to mix it up, explore new tools, and learn a few new tricks each time you try something new.

The Microsoft Education toolkit offers so many tools to make communication in our educational settings not only effective but also fun.

Everyone Matters: Communicating Using Immersive Reader

Before we go any further into discussions and examples of communication, we really want to highlight Microsoft's commitment to making sure all kinds of communication are accessible to all people in terms of reading, writing, listening, and speaking. Microsoft created this brilliant piece of assistive technology called Immersive Reader that is now an embedded component of so many Microsoft applications—and even used by several partner apps as well.

Microsoft's mission statement is "to empower every person and organization on the planet to achieve more." Mike Tholfsen, principal product manager for Microsoft Education, is famous for proudly proclaiming that Immersive Reader is "built-in, mainstream, non-stigmatizing, and free." That last point is critical: Microsoft's Immersive Reader is free—completely free—for everyone in the world. This is not a special license, or a paid service, or a subscription. Even if you wouldn't consider your school a "Microsoft school" (with teachers and students who use mostly Microsoft tools), you can still use Immersive Reader.

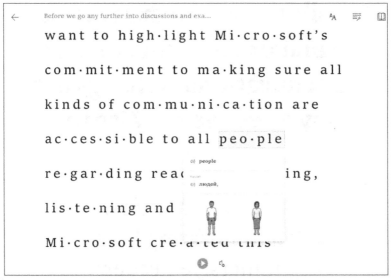

That last paragraph shown in Immersive Reader, with syllabification, picture dictionary, translation, text spacing, font selection, and Read Aloud all in place to support a wide variety of readers.

When Immersive Reader was first released a few years ago, it was available as an add-in that needed to be downloaded. Kathi remembers explaining its functionality to her IT department and requesting that it be installed on district devices. They asked for a list of all students who needed accommodations so they could install it, and Kathi emphatically replied that *everyone* needed this installed— every student and teacher in the district. She knew that it would benefit everyone for different reasons at different times.

Hector Minto, a Microsoft accessibility expert from England, often talks about three levels of disability: permanent, temporary, and situational. During his talks, he shows three photos. The first is of an amputee with one arm, someone who is permanently disabled. The next is a child with a cast on one arm, someone who is temporarily disabled. The third and final image is of a parent carrying a baby in one arm, someone who is situationally disabled. Hector speaks about how we all face challenges at different times: we might find it hard to read if we forget our glasses and the print is small; we may have a hard time hearing our phone in a noisy place; we could have trouble focusing due to noise or even lighting; or we might travel to a place where we can't read or speak the language. His message is profound. We all experience moments in which we need some help to access information or to communicate.

Immersive Reader provides that help. Any user can turn it on at any time and benefit from whichever of the following capabilities they may need to adjust or enable: text size, spacing, or font; background/text color; syllabication of words; highlighting of various parts of speech; a line focus reader; a picture dictionary; and a translation tool that will turn any word or an entire document into any of over sixty languages.

We wholeheartedly believe in teaching *all* students how to use Microsoft's Immersive Reader. This is not just a tool to help students who require accommodations. All students—everyone—can benefit from knowing that there are tools like this built into their computers or devices.

Get ready to set sail: Try out Immersive Reader on your own. Visit microsoft.com/learningtools from your favorite web browser to see it in action. Then open Word, OneNote, Flipgrid, Wakelet, Outlook, Forms, Minecraft, and more to see the Immersive Reader icon displayed (or check the View ribbon). Open Immersive Reader in the View ribbon in Office apps or look for the Immersive Reader icon in other apps to launch it. You might be amazed how comfortable it is for readers of all types.

Let's Get This Party Started: Communicating Using Microsoft Translator

We mentioned translation tools earlier, and it's worth pausing to explain how Microsoft Translator can play an essential role in breaking down translation barriers to communication.

As an educator in the Kent School District in Washington, USA, Becky had a personal passion for ensuring that students and families have access to translation services both during the school day and beyond. The district, which covers a seventy-square-mile area about ten miles south of Seattle, contains farmland, urban sprawl, estate homes in gated communities, manufacturing centers, apartment complexes, and even a refugee center. There are over 140 languages spoken in the district, and Becky has experienced that diversity firsthand as a classroom teacher. She once had a student from an island in the Federated States of Micronesia. He was Chuukese, and there aren't that many people *in the world* who speak the Chuukese language. Getting interpretation services for every child and family can call for some creative solutions.

You might have a similar situation in your own school, and you might know just how hard it is to find interpretation services. School districts never have enough interpreters, and those who are on staff are burdened with more need than they can cover. Many times, this means that a family won't have access to their student's teacher that day.

Becky has a personal experience with Translator that is best told in her own words:

> When I was managing our district-wide learning management system, I asked our student information system manager if I could have a report of the top ten languages spoken by the families in our school district. I also asked what percentage of our families would be supported if I enabled those ten language packs inside our learning management system. At the time, the answer was eighty percent. Eighty percent of our families would be supported in their native language with just ten languages enabled! I was floored. What an easy decision! I turned on those ten language packs the next day. At least most of our students were able to view the navigation features inside the website in their native language, even if they couldn't view the content that way. Browser-based translation extensions hadn't surfaced yet, so students were left to copy and paste content into translation websites as needed. That took time, executive function skills, and an internet connection—something many of the students didn't always have.
>
> When Microsoft Translator started emerging as a true solution for classrooms and teachers, I knew I wanted to be involved. Translator had been added to tools like OneNote and Word, so students could translate on the fly, and it was even built into Immersive Reader fairly early on. I was excited to show schools the impact of having the Translator app running in their classrooms, on their smartphones, and during parent interactions.

I was thrilled to be asked to be a part of one video project to showcase the amazing impact that Translator can have in a school, and I immediately asked the middle school I had worked in previously if we could document students using Translator. The principal said yes, but she wanted to make sure the video showed authentic use. She asked if we would help train her teachers on using Translator with student and parents as well. It was a perfect solution! Some of the videos at Translator for Education (aka.ms/TranslatorEDU) are the product of that partnership—one in which students and teachers got access to a tool to help build relationships, access information, and communicate more clearly.

Microsoft Translator has a whole group of services that teachers everywhere should know about, even if they don't have the same diversity of language as Becky did. Translator can be used strictly in English as a captioning or transcription tool. It can add captions to meetings or even create a transcript for a classroom conversation. Many people benefit from having access to subtitles, captioning, or live transcription, from individuals whose first language isn't the dominant language in the room to those with hearing impairments. Some professional development sessions even use

Two-person view of the Translator app, with English and Spanish selected. Just set your mobile device on the table between you and the person with whom you are speaking, and press the microphone icon to get started.

Translator as a back-channel chatroom. Participants join the conversation, post in their preferred language, and see the responses in the chat in their preferred language as well.

Our favorite use of Translator is through the mobile app. The mobile app is simple and allows teachers to have real-time conversations with someone who does not share their language. Office assistants, principals, teachers, and coaches are all using the mobile app to ensure that students and families can communicate. It's a great tool to have in your pocket, even when traveling! Scan and translate signs, menus, and images straight from the app to help navigate your personal adventures.

Russell White, principal at Chinook Middle School in Clyde Hill, Washington, USA, has made the best use of the tool. Chinook Middle School's nine hundred students (ages eleven to fourteen) speak thirty-two different languages. Four times a year, Russell hosts multilanguage coffee chats with parents, in which he provides interpreters for each of his four major language groups. Parents arrange themselves at tables by languages, with the appropriate interpreter at each one, and then he leads a discussion. While Russell liked the human connection that sitting in small groups brought to the events, he noticed a few things he didn't like. His groups grew larger, and soon the parents couldn't all fit at the tables. There were accuracy concerns using volunteer translators who were all trying to listen and manage a table at once. He couldn't expand the offering to additional language groups because he didn't have enough volunteer interpreters. And he was concerned about the way he had to offer a separate event for these families. It felt inequitable to him that they weren't getting the information at the same time as the English-speaking families.

One evening Russell hit his tipping point. A mother walked into the coffee chat and looked around at his predetermined tables, labeled in the languages for each one. "Where is the Russian table?" she asked. Russell didn't have a Russian table because he didn't have a Russian interpreter. He apologized and invited her to sit down anyway. She did, but she left partway through, and he never saw her at the school again. "I was literally sick to my stomach," he recalled to me when we talked. "I had done so much, but it still wasn't enough. It's not about the number impacted; it's about each person as an individual."

Russell teamed up with his school district's IT director and came up with a plan for a manageable way for *all* parents to get the access they needed at one parent night. They brought in a Bluetooth microphone and tested out Translator. They had parents install the app before the parent night using instructions they sent home in the families' self-identified preferred languages. When the parents arrived at the school, the staff members helped them join the conversation. And then the magic happened. Parents could read or listen to Russell's information in their own languages, and they could post or dictate questions back in their own languages. In total, eight languages were represented that night. The use of Translator completely changed the environment and allowed everyone to feel equally connected to the school. To Russell, this aligned perfectly with their district strategic goal to engage families and community members systemically.

Building from the Ground Up: Communicating Using Minecraft

Monika Limmer, an educator at Allenvale School in Christchurch, New Zealand, talked to us about her use of Minecraft: Education Edition with a different group who had difficulty in communicating. Her group of students have a range of physical and cognitive abilities, and some of them are nonverbal and use an augmentative and alternative communication (AAC) device. This presents lots of challenges for students to be able to show their thinking. After attending a training, Monika decided to try Minecraft with her students despite being "no Minecraft wizard" herself.

What happened next blew Monika away. Her often reserved students started teaching each other—and their teachers—by sharing techniques and ideas and connecting their projects to prior learning. These students began practicing communication skills with true purpose (via helping someone) and an authentic audience (i.e., a classmate needing help). Students became more self-directed because they had ownership over their building goals, and they supported each other with tips when they got stuck.

The in-game chat function quickly surfaced as an incredible asset for this group of learners. More reluctant students began writing more frequently because they could use the chat to communicate with their collaborators inside the game. These are students who wouldn't have felt comfortable or didn't have the physical ability to share verbally, but, thanks to chat messages, they became active members of the project.

Monika shared the story of one student who is nonverbal and had been a bit left out by some of the other students in the past. Minecraft proved to be just the ticket for unlocking his expertise and increased his "cool factor" with the other students, who began actively asking him for help—and not just in Minecraft.

Most important of all, Monika has observed that her students can contribute on a variety of levels according to their own ability and then showcase their understanding in a way that fits their learning goals. "The growth in self-esteem has been awesome to see," she commented. Her students have adopted a new mindset that they are capable of finishing a task that others find impressive, which means they are more willing to communicate about that work with others—through whatever type of communication tool they have.

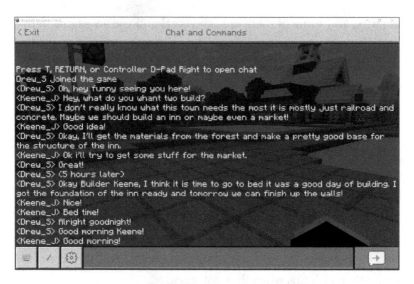

Two young builders working together via Minecraft chat.
Just press T in the game to access the chat.

A Slide Is Worth a Thousand Words: Communicating Using PowerPoint

Since the inception of the Office suite, people the world over have been using PowerPoint to share colorful, thematic presentations with their intended audiences. Students love to personalize their presentations with fonts, images, animations, transitions, hyperlinks, 3D images, digital ink, and more. Yet communicating a clear message through PowerPoint presentations is something that most people don't do well naturally.

There are quite literally millions of websites giving users information on how to create more effective PowerPoints. But toggling between them and your PowerPoint can be clunky. Plus, there's nothing out there to help you give a better presentation, which involves not just your PowerPoint presentation but also you speaking—at least there wasn't anything until Microsoft released Presenter Coach.

Presenter Coach is an artificial intelligence–powered technology assistant that can help teachers and students prepare for presentations without standing in front of a real audience just yet. It's freely available in PowerPoint Online for anyone to try.

Launch Presenter Coach using the View ribbon in PowerPoint Online. Choose View, then Rehearse with Coach.

Presenter Coach works by listening to your voice as you present, scanning the slide for content, and determining what you may need to work on. Note that your voice isn't being recorded; Microsoft has always been on the conservative side of student data privacy and your students' words aren't being stored in a cloud. But while the artificial intelligence is listening, it's providing real-time feedback to the speaker. The coach might give an on-screen prompt that the student is speaking too quickly or is reading off the slide instead of summarizing the content. The coach will also give suggestions for more inclusive language and keep track of filler statements like "um" or "basically." When finished, the student receives a report of their progress.

The progress report is a tidy way to get all sorts of information about the practice. Our favorite part of the report is the Rehearse Again button. It's a great reminder for students and adults alike that communication skills come with practice.

This example rehearsal report shows the categories that will appear in any report. Ever wonder what filler words you use? Try it out!

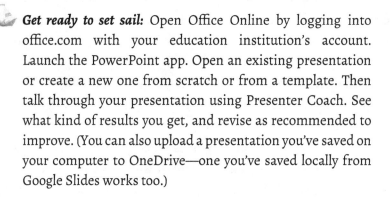

Get ready to set sail: Open Office Online by logging into office.com with your education institution's account. Launch the PowerPoint app. Open an existing presentation or create a new one from scratch or from a template. Then talk through your presentation using Presenter Coach. See what kind of results you get, and revise as recommended to improve. (You can also upload a presentation you've saved on your computer to OneDrive—one you've saved locally from Google Slides works too.)

Go Ahead, Make My Sway: Communicating Using Sway

Skilled communication at its best means students are producing extended, multimodal communication that is designed for a specific audience and includes supporting evidence. This is much different than the decades-old practice of having students stand in front of the class reading off PowerPoint slides.

Effective communication isn't just exchanging information. It is important that the sender conveys emotions, voice, and intent while the receiver processes all inputs to gain full meaning. That's probably why people started using graphics and changing fonts inside newsletters, slide shows, and print publications. Designers know that the colors and branding included in a finished product can ultimately influence the viewer.

One of our favorite tools to communicate a message is Sway. People sometimes ask how Sway is different than PowerPoint . . . or Prezi, or Google Slides, or any other web-based creation tool, for that matter. One of Sway's features that stands out to us is the linear fluidity. There aren't sections broken up by slides, content presented in pieces, or chunky transitions, which is why we love Sway for storytelling. It feels smoother than other platforms as we swipe through a page and watch text and images float in to support the text in a scrolling, subtly animated flow.

It's powerful to witness students using Sway to tell their stories, design presentations, and demonstrate their understanding of a topic. At the same time, many teachers use Sway for distributing their own content. In fact, one of the top uses for Sway in the entire world is class newsletters. Sway's simple design tools, ability to add rich media content, and mobile accessible format make it perfect for this purpose. Many teachers share a weekly link through their favorite classroom communication method. Because Sway is web-based, these newsletters can be edited from any device with an internet connection; this includes uploading photos from a mobile device on the fly.

Julie Fletcher, a literacy teacher at Ysgol Gyfun Y Strade in Llanelli, Wales, uses Sway to build her students' understanding of the writing process. Julie was working with a challenging group of students preparing to take their national exams, and they weren't using the resources she'd provided for them to help improve their writing. Her students were interested in gaming, media, and mobile content.

She decided to give Sway a try, and she first used the import feature to move her Word documents and PowerPoint presentations into Sway. Julie was pleasantly surprised at the easy transfer—it only took her a few minutes per import to format the Sway and have it ready for her students.

Sway's Class Newsletter template is a great way to get started. Choose the template from Sway's start page at sway.com and begin editing to add your own details, images, and style.

Julie gave the URL for each new resource to her students, which immediately gave them better access on their mobile devices. Because of the view counts available in Sway's dashboard, Julie knew that her students were accessing them. Her students also commented that the tasks and descriptions included in the Sways had a greater flow—a "trajectory of learning" that was smooth instead of segmented. Julie used the headings in Sway to create a topic-based menu system within the Sway, so students could anchor themselves to their current task without being distracted by other sections, helping to personalize the learning experience.

Perhaps the best part of Julie's story is when a student in her class told her that he wouldn't be viewing her Sways at all. He told her that reading was difficult, and he preferred not to look at them. Julie took a risk and asked the student to make her a deal: if she recorded all of the content of each Sway in a podcast format, would he listen to them? The student said he would. So, Julie set off with a new idea. Using the built-in screencasting and recording tool in Windows (accessible by pressing the Windows key and G together), she recorded her Sways with her own descriptions and audio. She made all seven Sways from her writing unit into video mini-lessons and gave her students access to those links as well.

What happened next was certainly a surprise—about 90 percent of her students accessed the video mini-lessons! She began to see increased assignment submission, increased engagement during class time, and students submitting digital work with less guidance. Her students reported that they could listen to the videos while they flipped through the Sway on their mobile devices, or they could simply listen to her talk with their earbuds in and claim to be listening to music instead to avoid being stigmatized within their peer group. Julie notes that students who learn best in a traditional environment already have plenty of access to whatever they need, so "we have to create new ways to reach all the other learners more creatively." Julie's ability to communicate with her students in a way that worked best for them is making a difference for her students both now and in their futures.

One of the most powerful uses of Sway we have ever come across originates with our colleague Lee Whitmarsh, who was an art teacher at Alsager's School in the small town of Alsager, England, before moving to Australia in 2019. A town full of empathetic residents, Alsager decided to become dementia friendly. When the local media outlet approached the school for an idea of how to get started, Lee first had some simple ideas, like creating a mural or painting to inspire others. But then he realized something important: a mural on the wall is static, bringing awareness but nothing more. Lee was inspired by what he called "a swirl in my head" to utilize Sway to create portable, flexible artifacts that would make a difference for the lives of those coping with dementia.

Lee started with the concept of reminiscence therapy, which is when people who have been diagnosed with dementia are exposed to a combination of imagery, sound, and touch to help unlock long-term memories and find solace in the recollection. Many people, he noted, had boxes of photos and memorabilia in their homes that went untouched. Through a partnership with a local community organization, Lee organized three couples (each consisting of one person with dementia and their partner) to come into the school as a pilot program. His students offered the couples tea or coffee and biscuits and simply sat and talked at the first meeting. They explained their project, which was to make a digital story of the person's memories. They then asked if the couples would return with their memory boxes from home and work with them to create the digital story. The students had previously created biographical Sways of artists, so they were able to show the couples some samples of what the final product might look like.

When the couples returned, they brought boxes of trinkets, artifacts, and photos with them. Students led interviews to ask questions about the content, digitized it using photos and scanners, and added context like music, videos, or maps. The students began by creating art collages about the couples' lives. Since collage is a standard art portfolio project at the school, students were completing an assignment while asking the couples questions about their histories. They found that the person diagnosed with dementia would sometimes be able to share information that had never been shared before: a smell, something said, or a flavor that reminded them of their past.

Finally, the couples returned to edit the Sways alongside the student. Each piece of the story was a collaborative work. Along the way, students showed the partner without dementia how to edit the Sway in the future. Each family member was given an editing link to the Sway so they could add to it and a view link to access on their mobile devices. They later heard reports of people in the project swiping through their Sway over and over, telling stories on the best days and seeking comfort from familiarity on others.

Go check out some of these Sway Life Stories on the website swaylifestories.com.

Looking back, Lee noted that making the Sway for the family was an important project, but the stronger result was the dynamic between the school and the community that the project created. Students bump into these couples in the community and have a connection to another generation. They accessed deep social emotional intelligence throughout the project and were able to positively impact another human being. Beyond the awards and recognitions this project has received is an important lesson: mutually creative ownership gives people without a voice a way to find their inner self again.

Show What You Know: Communicating Using Microsoft Forms

It's important that students communicate what they know with their teachers, yet students often don't understand the value of communicating their thinking. It's true that communicating understanding isn't an easy task. One must take the multitude of thoughts rumbling around in one's brain and categorize, organize, and simplify them. Most students need to be taught this process, and the learning begins when they are still young.

One way that students share their grasp of concepts, ideas, and skills throughout the school year is through a variety of assessments. Formative assessments give educators an opportunity to understand what students know, what students don't know, and where they might have misconceptions or errors in their thinking. Summative assessments allow educators to assign standards-based scores or mastery grades to student work, which is required by most school systems for reporting purposes and identifying students of concern. In a project-based classroom, teachers often spend most of their time helping students reach their goals and conferencing with students about their progress.

Microsoft Forms is a simple platform that gives teachers an opportunity to evaluate student understanding, but that's not it's only focus. We'd also like to highlight the opportunity it gives students to communicate their thinking through a variety of inputs. Students using Forms can answer questions formatted as multiple choice and multiple answer, but there is also the opportunity for short answers or a text box. Think about how the short answer space can be used. In Microsoft Forms, students can submit text or a math equation, but they can also submit a link to *anything* that lives on the

68

internet: a Flipgrid video response, a Whiteboard sketch note, a file stored in OneDrive, or even a blog post.

There are a couple of ways that Forms can be used to help students communicate their understanding to themselves. There's an old saying: "You don't know what you don't know." Teachers can use Forms to create branching questions to help students build an awareness of their own growth areas or challenges. Branching means that if a student answers a multiple-choice question with answer A, he or she will see another question below that is designed to follow-up answer A. But if the student responds with answer B, he or she will see a different follow-up question. There is huge potential in designing student activities this way. If a student responds to a question by selecting a common misconception as his or her answer, for example, the teacher can redirect this thinking through a video, image, text, or other additional information in the follow-up question. The student then receives instant awareness of their level of understanding of the topic.

We know a science teacher who uses branching Forms with students to help them understand their own growth areas and improve them. Prior to every science unit, she gives a pre-assessment, which is full of questions about topics that would have been covered in previous years of school and are building blocks to understand

Microsoft Forms can be used on any device with an internet connection.

the concepts in the upcoming unit. This formative assessment is particularly useful since a significant number of students have not spent their careers in the same school system, and the teacher can't count on their prior knowledge being the same. This teacher's students frequently comment that they are thankful to have a chance to start a unit with the same background as everyone else. Ultimately, these students are more successful because they understand their own knowledge base, and the gaps in their understanding have been communicated to them through Forms.

Another amazing use for Forms is to communicate social-emotional needs. You may have seen pictures or clips of teachers asking students to assess their "mood of the day" as they enter a classroom. While we love the emphasis on student emotion and the impact it can have on their days at school, we always wonder if students truly feel comfortable sharing that information publicly. In a scenario in which students each have access to a device (mobile or otherwise), a teacher can use Forms to collect this information quickly and privately. And the same Form can be used day after day to gather new information and track trends in student moods.

 Get ready to set sail: You've likely heard of Google Forms, but have you tried Microsoft Forms? It's a great tool that is securely nestled in the Office 365 platform. It also includes the best tools for accessibility we've seen, like translation, branching, and Immersive Reader. Open Office Online by logging into office.com with your education institution's account. Launch the Forms app. Test out a Form or a Quiz for an upcoming formative assessment. Share with your students or colleagues, then return to the Forms app for the results.

Teams Really Do Come True: Communicating Using Microsoft Teams

In Kathi's school district, she works under many administrators in many different capacities. One of her bosses is named Ginny Grier, a principal at Bells Elementary School. Ginny recently decided that she wanted to be purposeful about improving her edtech skills and lead by example. Of course, we're thrilled anytime someone feels "tech-venturous," and administrators don't often prioritize their own edtech personal development. But when administrators model and use technology in communicating with their teachers, the teachers follow suit and start finding creative ways to use it in their classrooms. This was an amazing opportunity for a whole-school change.

When administrators model and use technology in communicating with their teachers, the teachers follow suit and start finding creative ways to use it in their classrooms.

Kathi taught Ginny about Microsoft Teams, and Ginny was enthralled. She set up a Bells School Team, where in addition to the "general" channel for all school staff, she has a private channel for each of the grade levels 1–5, as well as for special area teachers, special education teachers, basic skills teachers, and office staff.

She wanted her teachers to be trained on the basics and almost "forced" to use it to access certain things. So, in the general channel's conversation area, the first thing she added was a video screencast. It was a two-minute basic overview of how Microsoft Teams works. She wanted that to be the first thing her teachers saw. After that, she posted a silly question in the conversation area and asked people to just try Teams by clicking the Reply button. Her third and last post in this conversation area directed everyone to the Files tab, in which she had two resources about how to manage notifications in Teams. This communication was all intentional: it was a clever way to get teachers to explore the Teams ecosystem, try responding to a fun prompt and see others' responses, and find something in the Files section.

The following week, Ginny asked teachers to post a favorite quote to each other in their private group channel. Ginny went in and responded to many of the quotes that were posted. She also asked everyone to post in the general conversation area one GIF about how their work week was going. The staff had a great time seeing and replying to each others' posts, and they found emoji and some other fun things as they got more comfortable exploring. Ginny kept the entire Teams experience lighthearted and not at all intimidating. Staff learned more on their own and began talking about ways they could use this in their classrooms.

Ginny also wanted to revamp the way afternoon announcements are done. Normally, as buses pulled up, the secretary called each bus number over the school's speaker system. When Ginny saw the video capability in Teams, she and her very lively secretaries decided it was time to make dismissal more visible and fun. She created a new channel called Dismissal, and at the end of each day, one of the office staff members appears in costume or with photo props as they post bus numbers on a whiteboard. All classroom teachers simply click on that channel and hit Join Now, and they can see the office staff doing live video dismissal. Even with the volume turned down, everyone in the classrooms can see all of the posted bus numbers, and nobody wants to miss the super silly afternoon dismissal crew. In the future, Ginny has plans to add student newscasters so they can live-broadcast school announcements.

Not Another Meeting: Communicating Using Flipgrid

Perhaps most impressive was an idea that Ginny came up with on her own. She wanted to do faculty meetings in a different way that was more respectful of her teachers' time, so she decided to use Flipgrid as her communication tool. In fact, she decided to deliver all of her faculty meeting content via Flipgrid. She makes videos of the necessary things she needs to communicate with her teachers and posts them as monthly videos the teachers can access whenever they have the time. Using Flipgrid, staff can respond or ask questions via video response.

She added a new tab to her general channel in Teams, and now her Flipgrid faculty meeting tab is right at the top of her Team. If anyone wants to ask questions, share some news, or further elaborate on points from the faculty "meeting," they also have the option to post text-based answers in the channel.

We are so thrilled about the impact this one administrator has made on her school. Her faculty has so much respect for how she chose Flipgrid to value their time. Communication is at an all-time high, and teachers are clamoring to learn how to use these tools and features.

This is the home page of the Bells Faculty Meeting Flipgrid. There are drop-down topics for each month of the school year, where Ginny Grier posts a video of everything she wants to say as her "faculty meeting," and staff members can respond right within the topic by adding Flipgrid videos of their own.

Teachers who hadn't used Flipgrid now love it and realize how easy and powerful it is as a communication tool to use with students. Some classroom teachers have begun trying Teams with their students. Teachers love the live video camera, so they're using that to create and communicate with colleagues in Teams they create themselves. All of this growth and innovation is happening because one person had a spark of interest in a new delivery model and a calling to be a true digital leader.

 Get ready to set sail: Consider a piece of information that you would normally deliver in person or by text delivery (email, newsletter, post, etc.). Modify the message to be delivered via Teams Live Meeting or by Flipgrid video to be viewed anytime. See what kind of feedback and engagement you get from your audience . . . and how it changes the way you communicate.

Only a Phone Call Away:
Communicating Using Skype
in the Classroom

It seems appropriate to end a chapter on communication with a discussion of Skype in the Classroom, which is obviously an incredibly powerful communication tool. You've already seen how Skype in the Classroom can be leveraged for collaboration, and in the upcoming chapters you'll see it used in a variety of different ways to achieve other Cs in conjunction with communication. But what impresses us most about this next story is how Skype in the Classroom is used as a communication tool that has the added effect of teaching students empathy.

Emma Nääs, a teacher of ten- and eleven-year-old students at Jonslundsskola in Gothenburg, Sweden, teaches in a small town of just three hundred. Many of the students live on farms that their families have held for centuries, and the community is very locally grounded. Emma decided that her students needed to experience life outside of the community, just to see what else there was to see in the world. Focusing on writing with question words (a literacy lesson), her students would write a list of questions for "An Interview with a Stranger." Knowing that the questions would actually be put to use, her students wrote forty-one questions together instead of the usual five they had written in previous years before they had an authentic purpose. Emma then wrote a letter to someone she knew in Spain and asked if her students could send him a list of questions. She received a reply that he was a bit too busy for a letter but could set up a Skype call. The call worked out, and her students got to ask their questions.

From that day on, Emma knew that was the right path. She wrote to people all over the world—three hundred people, many of whom are not educators but whom she had met as an exchange student and on a professional visitation trip, asking if her students could interview them over Skype. Because the Skype in the Classroom platform is free and available for any internet-capable device with a camera and microphone, it just made sense. Emma has found that Skype in the Classroom sessions with her students have led them to have greater appreciation for others and increased empathy for those they've never met.

Emma's class recently completed a project in which they connected with other schools to share a cultural or traditional song via Skype in the Classroom. She shared a story with us in which her students connected with another school but couldn't hear the person playing the song, as they had moved too far away from the microphone. "Let's not tell them," her students whispered together. Emma's students listened for an entire three minutes, rapt with attention, and then clapped voraciously as if they had heard the entire performance. When Emma asked them about it later, they explained their thinking. "It didn't make sense to interrupt," they replied. "And we would have been so embarrassed if that had happened to us. It was

W better to honor the musician than point it out."

Having educator friends from around the world inevitably leads to global opportunities for students, as you'll see in the story of Tammy Dunbar, one of the educators Emma reached out to. Tammy is a fifth-grade (students ages ten to eleven) teacher in Manteca Unified School District in Manteca, California, USA. She has fully embraced the Microsoft Education tools, which has led to many amazing experiences for both her and her students.

I did a "mirrored classroom" with Emma Nääs in Sweden. We both read *Number the Stars* by Lois Lowry and decided to do a book study, but in deciding to be mirror classrooms, we took things a step further. I was like a supplemental teacher to her classroom, and she was one to mine. With the time difference,

I was at home to introduce myself. "Hi, I'm Mrs. Dunbar. I'm going to be your second teacher," I said, and she did the same. Then together both classes did a group Sway. We did a "cover walk" to predict what the book would be about, and we learned that their cover in Sweden is *way* different than our cover. We started learning together right away. We even recreated scenes in Minecraft at one point, and those were put up on the Sway. We created a story in PowerPoint for them with a video of my students reading it, but we also turned on the captions, and we illustrated it. Then they sent us back a PowerPoint of them doing all the same things, but reading the story in English, because they had learned how from watching us!

Now my students are so used to this that they don't think twice about asking, "Hey, can we reach out to a Global Mentor with our Minecraft question?" After hearing that there was an earthquake in Japan, they asked, "Is our friend Mio okay? Maybe we should check." Suddenly, world events mean something to them. The places have meaning because they know people who are there, and they don't think a thing about reaching out to someone outside of the classroom to get help.

Suddenly, world events mean something to them.

These shared experiences have brought their students closer together as a class and established connections with those around the world. Tammy shared one more story illustrating how Skype in the Classroom serves as a powerful motivator for change.

Thanks to the Skype in the Classroom website, I found and joined a global project called World Wonder Day, and my class paired with a class in Greece. The focus that year was hunger, and the idea was that we would study hunger in our community, they would study hunger in their community, and then we would use Skype in the Classroom to talk about what we had found out and what we could do to combat it. My students learned that Second Harvest Food Bank fed about a thousand people in our community of seventy thousand. It just so happens that about 82 percent of my students qualify for free or reduced lunch, so food insecurity is not a theoretical issue for them. We reported that to Greece, and we started brainstorming with them about what we could do.

It happened to be that pre-holiday time of year when canned food drives are happening. My students saw the flyers around town and said that our school should get involved. Our classroom had a window that was on a major street in town, so the kids made this giant sign that said, "Help Us Feed the Hungry." Then they did some calculations after asking Second Harvest Food Bank how many canned goods it took to feed a family of four for a day. As items came in, they started stacking them in our windows so people could see, and soon the students were exclaiming, "We've already raised enough to feed two families for a day" . . . and then five families for a day, and it just kept growing.

Then my students said that they wanted to do even *more* and wondered how they could get the word out to ask for more help. They wanted to know if someone would come out to write an article for a newspaper, but instead I encouraged them to write it and submit it themselves. I had kids excited to write because it was for a real newspaper, a real audience, and a great cause. So, I had a little group of five girls that wrote a press release. We went through the whole editing process, and then they submitted it, and got it in the local paper! Because of this, we *tripled* what the school had done the year before. The kids were out there when Second Harvest came to pick up our twenty-seven boxes of canned and dry goods. I then had a class of fifth graders exclaiming, "We just fed a ton of people! What else can we do? What's next?"

It blew me away to see the power of that one little tiny global connection. We reached out to our friends in Greece and told them what we did, and they had had similar results! It was just so exciting to see students on two different continents seeing how big an impact they could make on the world. Helping to create students who are global citizens is one of the most amazing opportunities that I've gotten to see firsthand through Microsoft.

Emma and Tammy have found that the foundational principles of geography, writing, communication, and citizenship are so much more relevant to students when they are addressed in authentic ways within experiential learning. "Skip the sparkly gadgets and bring experiences into your classroom," Emma advises, "things that you know in your heart will fit in your classroom with the goals that you need to accomplish anyway. When you teach like that, you'll always end up teaching more than you planned."

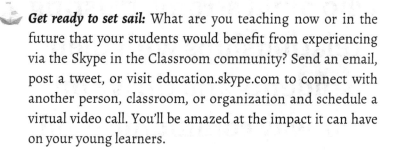 ***Get ready to set sail:*** What are you teaching now or in the future that your students would benefit from experiencing via the Skype in the Classroom community? Send an email, post a tweet, or visit education.skype.com to connect with another person, classroom, or organization and schedule a virtual video call. You'll be amazed at the impact it can have on your young learners.

Conclusion

Throughout this book, we share so many stories of teachers who are exemplary communicators. Using these Microsoft Education tools, these kinds of teachers make all of the other Cs possible. They need to communicate to have a community, to collaborate, to unleash creativity, to challenge critical thinking, and to encourage computational thinking. We obviously could include any of these teachers' stories in this chapter, but we want to encourage you to read on and learn about how they are leveraging communication to achieve additional Cs.

All these stories have their origins in listening to students, and the *best* teachers are those who build strong, trusting relationships with their students and thrive on two-way communication. They are excellent listeners. Carl Rogers is credited with saying, "We think we listen, but very rarely do we listen with real understanding, true empathy. Yet listening, of this very special kind, is one of the most potent forces for change that I know."

The *best* teachers are those who build strong, trusting relationships with their students and thrive on two-way communication.

All teachers are more effective when they employ intentional, interpersonal, two-way communication. One such teacher is Luis Oliveira. Luis is an English language learners (ELL) support teacher for students ages fourteen to eighteen at Middletown High School in Middletown, Rhode Island, USA. He has found powerful ways to not just instruct his students but also connect with them in the most empathetic ways. Below, he tells the story of the impact Microsoft Education tools, such as Teams, Immersive Reader, Microsoft Translator, and Flipgrid, are having on his students. They are quite literally changing their lives by enabling them to communicate.

> To help these students get acclimated, to learn, and even to survive, I'm using a variety of Microsoft Tools, and it's been a game-changer. I was using an assortment of tools to help my kids, and there would be a log-on for this tool and a log-on for that tool. Flipgrid had its log-on, and Newsela had its log-on, and Go Formative had its log-on, and so on. With Microsoft Teams, I've been able to incorporate the tools that I love to use and to help my kids, but with one environment and with one log-on. Because some of my students have never touched a computer, the simpler I can make that transitional time and their experience with the technology, the easier it is for them. They'll be more comfortable and have a better chance at using the tools effectively.
>
> Within Microsoft Teams, the Immersive Reader is key. You talk about communication being one of those seven Cs that we're targeting, well, communication is number one for me. If the students can't communicate, either in written form or oral form, then they can't survive. They can't function. Teachers don't know what their students know if they can't get it out.
>
> In the old days, we'd have to wait to communicate with students who didn't have the language skills necessary—sometimes for only three months but for as long as one year or more for the students who had literacy issues in their first language. Now,

I can put the students on Microsoft Translator, and they can translate everything to begin communicating immediately.

On Friday, we were playing around with Microsoft PowerPoint and the ability to use subtitles, and the kids were floored. They thought this was so cool! We discussed how their teachers could just have that up while doing their normal lecture, and the students who don't know English can see what the teacher is saying—and vice versa. The student can do a presentation in their first language, with subtitles in English, and the teacher can see what the student knows. That's amazing.

Oh, and of course we use Flipgrid with Immersive Reader. It makes life so much easier. The biggest feature of Flipgrid that I've been using is the MixTape. I'm able to create a MixTape for each one of my kids, and throughout the year I'm able to take their September videos and put them in their MixTape, then their October videos, and so forth. Then I can see, and more important, *they* can see their growth over time. That has been huge, because one of the difficulties that we sometimes see is that the students don't think they're learning. Often, they don't believe that they're getting better, and they think that their English is horrible, and they don't want anyone to hear. But I sit them in front of the computer, and I say, "Play your September video. Do you notice that you did that one all in Spanish? And now it's January and look, your videos are now in English, and they're getting better and better! There's more depth and more vocabulary, and the content is more descriptive." And they say, "Oh wow, I am getting better!" Once they realize that, that moment of recognition that they are learning, they tend to bloom and flourish and believe in themselves. And that's what we must have for the student to be a successful language learner. You've got to use the language.

Luis makes communication magic happen every day by empowering his students. Not only are they able to understand what they hear, but they are also being truly heard. Luis's students can show what they know, and the most beautiful part of this story is the growth in their confidence. Those students sail the Cs with Luis at the helm.

Communication Anchor Points

⚓ Use, promote, and train students on inclusive tools like Immersive Reader and Translator.

⚓ Model effective and varied communication practices that meet the needs of your audience.

⚓ Allow students to communicate their voice to you and others in a variety of methods.

Crew Member Spotlight: **Lee Whitmarsh**

Watch and listen as Lee Whitmarsh, who taught in England and now lives in Australia, shares his amazing story of impacting lives through communication.

Use your Flipgrid app to scan the QR code for an augmented reality experience or use any QR code reader to view as a standard video. You can also access the link to this video from the Wakelet collection for this chapter.

CREATORS

J ohn Harris, in his TEDx talk "How Students Become Creators Instead of Consumers of Technology," claims students need both courage and curiosity to not only use technology but also make it their own. He states that students need to be "inventors instead of duplicators, innovators instead of imitators," and enthusiastic pioneers in a globally competitive market. These are inspiring words! How do we get there?

It's more than just the maker movement. The maker movement has been all about letting students invent, create, and design physical objects as a sort of combination between hacking and build-it-yourself projects. The maker movement in schools has led to teachers hoarding cardboard, aluminum foil, tape, and wooden craft sticks so students can build prototypes and models. Sometimes maker activities are thematic or problem based, and sometimes they're open-ended tasks. The maker movement has certainly sparked the idea that students can create, but it's only a small piece of the overall picture.

Sometimes, scaffolding creative opportunities is just what students need to get started—to light that creative spark. For some students, open-ended is scary. The Use–Modify–Create recursive model focuses the design thinking tasks on moving from being a consumer of others' products to a creator, tester, and analyzer of new ideas. Students need exposure to the types of artifacts they will eventually create.

Playing games, reading books, watching videos, and controlling robots are all examples of using. Once students have experiences in these systems, they can begin to imagine how they might change the system to create something new. That's when students can design a game, write a story, film a movie, or build a robot. Then they can test, refine, and analyze their work product to improve upon their designs. As educators, we must provide students with experiences that build their internal repository so they can become creators.

How can we apply this ideology to student projects? What if we gave students fewer parameters and more open-ended opportunities? In the book *Creative Schools: The Grassroots Revolution That's Transforming Education* by Sir Ken Robinson and Lou Aronica, the authors help the reader understand that creativity "is not just about

What if we gave students fewer parameters and more open-ended opportunities?

having off-the-wall ideas and letting your imagination run free." Creativity, in fact, can involve "deep factual knowledge and high levels of practical skill." That becomes very evident when you investigate the different ways we can leverage Microsoft Education tools in the creative process.

Reduce, Reuse, Recycle: Creating Using Microsoft Templates

Let's start with the low-hanging fruit, which is actually quite tasty! Sometimes teachers have a task for students that's a little more specific than an open-ended project, or perhaps students have decided on their own project outcome but need some help getting started. When was the last time you checked out Office templates? It's a gold mine! Templates allow us to reduce our workload, reuse something that's already been created, and recycle a great idea.

Office templates are designed for Word, Excel, and PowerPoint and are available for Office Online or Office desktop apps. There are a wide variety of time-saving templates in the Education category based on common classroom practices. These templates are designed by educators for educators and students to use. Creating with efficiency is a huge benefit in today's busy world, and it's not often that we give ourselves the opportunity to simply modify an existing resource with our own information.

One of the things we love about templates is that it gives students a starting point. Instead of building designs, graphics, hyperlinks, formatting, and so on, students can focus on adding their content. They can create an artifact in a fraction of the time by customizing a template to meet their needs. It's super simple and frees up both instructional time and work time for students to focus on adding their thoughts instead of merging cells in a table. That's time well spent!

Access templates when you start a new Word document, PowerPoint presentation, or Excel spreadsheet through the Templates option when you choose New. You can also visit templates.office.com and search their Education category templates available for all three apps. You might find a time-saving template for yourself, like the hallway pass log or the playground safety guidelines. Office templates are a hidden gem when it comes to creating.

Search for Office templates in your favorite web browser, then filter for Education to access these resources.

A Guide by the Side: Creating Using QuickStarter

Creating an entire presentation or visual story from scratch can be daunting to many students (and teachers!) because of the executive function skills required. They must figure out the outline, format properly, bring in images, decide on design features, and then add content. Using QuickStarter allows students to forgo many of the smaller decisions involved in artifact creation, so they can focus on the content instead of the design elements.

QuickStarter is available in Sway or PowerPoint. You can give QuickStarter a topic, and the artificial intelligence server will figure out a set of subtopics that you might be interested in including in your presentation or visual story. QuickStarter doesn't do the research for the student and doesn't provide any written support materials, but it does give them direction on how to proceed.

Get ready to set sail: To see QuickStarter in action, have students open Sway and type the name of an animal into the Title Card. Then, have them click the Insert button to see all of the suggested photos, videos, and articles. Let them marvel at the artificial intelligence that is making their creative lives easier. To demonstrate how handy this QuickStarter is, set a time limit and ask students to see how far they can develop an animal report using various media. Of course, share some of those results, and let students reflect on using QuickStarter as a tool to jump-start a creative process.

Moving to the Third Dimension: Creating Using Paint 3D

There are several creator tools built into Windows 10 that don't get the attention they deserve. One that comes to mind immediately is Paint 3D. You may remember the Paint app if you've been a PC user for a while. Paint 3D is the significant upgrade that allows students to create 3D imagery.

The interface is simple to use and has tons of options to get kids excited. They can create illustrations for their writing, scenes from novels, pieces of history, interactive maps, scientific models, and mixed reality experiences. Paint 3D files can be added to PowerPoint, Word, or OneNote as manipulatable content and can be printed with a 3D printer. I'm not sure it gets more exciting for a young learner than building a 3D object on the computer, watching it be printed, and then holding it in their hand.

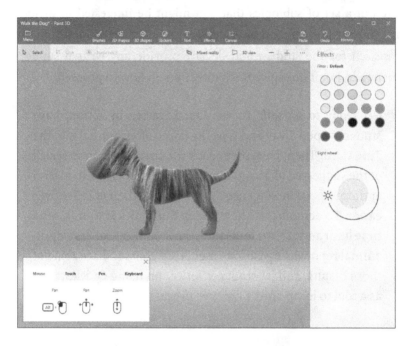

YouTube offers great tutorials for getting started with Paint 3D. Search "Paint 3D Creative Curriculum."

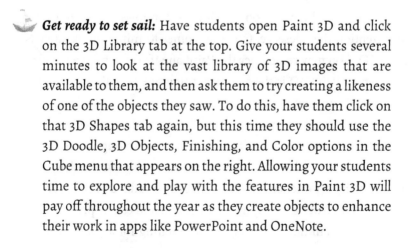 ***Get ready to set sail:*** Have students open Paint 3D and click on the 3D Library tab at the top. Give your students several minutes to look at the vast library of 3D images that are available to them, and then ask them to try creating a likeness of one of the objects they saw. To do this, have them click on that 3D Shapes tab again, but this time they should use the 3D Doodle, 3D Objects, Finishing, and Color options in the Cube menu that appears on the right. Allowing your students time to explore and play with the features in Paint 3D will pay off throughout the year as they create objects to enhance their work in apps like PowerPoint and OneNote.

Lights, Camera, Action!: Creating Using Video Editor

Windows 10 has a built-in Video Editor, and it's a wonderful addition to the set of creativity tools that are freely available to educators in the Microsoft suite. Video Editor allows students to add multiple **W** video clips, trim segments, and rearrange as needed. Students can add filters, text overlays, and motion, as well as background music or narration. The special effects are a student favorite.

When Becky taught fourth grade (ages nine to ten), she was invited by the future instructional technology department director (but technology coach at the time), Pat Regnart, to participate in Kent School District's visual literacy festival, called VisFest. It was an opportunity to let students tell their stories through film. There were themes and deadlines, and Becky wasn't sure if she could deviate that much from the spring curriculum to pull it off. Pat convinced her to enter anyway. He shared templates with her for teaching storyboarding, and off they went. Soon students were creating films about state history just to try it out.

The following year, Becky got serious about video. Her students had so much fun telling stories with video, so, with knowledge of that year's VisFest theme in hand, she planned to integrate the theme into the writing curriculum. Her students went through the entire writing process—brainstorming, drafting, revising, editing, peer review, and educator feedback—and then added the storyboarding layer on top. They talked about scenes and different types of shots. They learned about screenplay writing and how it is different from other forms of writing. Her budding screenplay writers recruited actors and videographers and then directed their own videos.

Postproduction work takes longer than you might think, especially if you're competing for a prize. Pat had warned Becky's class that one minute of published video usually took about ten hours of editing time if you had lots of trimming to do—and he was right! But in the end, the students submitted a few great videos to the festival, and one team was even recognized with an honorable mention in their age group (the only award given at VisFest) for their work. Most importantly, students saw themselves as creators. They had completed a creative work, start to finish. There is possibly nothing quite so satisfying as seeing a completed work after a long creative process.

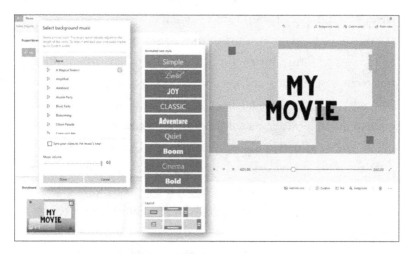

Windows Video Editor is built into any Windows 10 device.
Search for "Video Editor" or open the Photos app to
get started. You'll be surprised how easy it is.

We had the pleasure of speaking with Rebecca Demarest from the Bureau of Fearless Ideas (BFI) in Seattle, Washington, USA, recently. Rebecca is a writer-in-residence for the education programs at BFI, and she is positively passionate about teaching writing to urban, low-income middle-school students (ages eleven to fourteen). She is also passionate about using video. Rebecca discovered that with video, students could follow the entire writing process but with an added layer of engagement that couldn't be replicated in text.

She knows that video "gives students permission to engage with storytelling at a level that's more comfortable for a lot of kids today."

For a writing project that focused on speculative fiction, Rebecca lined up a field trip to the popular Museum of Pop Culture in Seattle Center. Her students visited the science fiction section of the museum for inspiration before beginning work on their stories. She knew that this type of inspiration would free her learners from being constrained to a certain genre and instead focus them on world building, plot construction, and character development.

Her students focus on the entire writing process and spend a lot of time playing with film before they write. Rebecca encourages her students to "play the movie in [their] mind" when they are writing their stories, and she actually gets to see those movies because students aren't being confined to text. Her learners are tackling topics like climate change and environmental responsibility through aliens living on Pizza Planet, and Microsoft's Video Editor allows them to add the special effects, sounds, narration, music, and themes they have in their heads.

Rebecca also points out that some of her students struggle with language skills (that's sometimes why they are in her workshops, after all), and she has noticed that students who have been diagnosed with dyslexia are often especially well-suited to a video project. Video removes the need for a story to be readable in print and the worry about putting words in the wrong order. It allows students to skip editing text and use imagery instead. She has noticed that these students, once free of the parameters of using strictly text, can finally begin to tell their stories.

 Get ready to set sail: If you want to see creative, engaged students, ask them to write a news story in the style of the game Two Truths and a Lie. Then have each student follow the writing process and storyboard his or her story to create a video. Students can use special effects to edit their videos and provide all sorts of entertaining additions to their work. Later, students can publish their videos to Microsoft Stream or Flipgrid for other students to view. The best part of this activity is having students guess which of the pieces of information in the news story are truths and which is a lie. Students can even leave comments on each other's videos in Stream and try to deduce which parts of the news stories are lies. This activity can lead into a lesson on fact-checking news stories released by local news agencies.

Not Your Mama's Slideshow: Creating Using PowerPoint

For years PowerPoint has been swept under the rug as an outdated, boring tool. So many other digital presentation tools have hit the market, and people love to grab for the fresh and new. And let's be honest: we have all seen some lousy PowerPoint presentations. But there are lots of lousy presentations using alternatives to PowerPoint too! Haven't we all sat through a few doozies with too many bullet points, too many words on the screen, or—worst of all—somebody reading every one of those too many words out loud to the audience? In the end, it comes down to how skilled the presenter is at creating delivering presentations.

But that was then. This, however, is not your mama's Office. If you haven't peeked at PowerPoint in a while, let us fill you in on a few new features that will rock your creative mind and make the art of creation so much simpler for you.

Before we continue, it's important to note that these features are available on the latest version of Office 365 on a Windows device. To access this feature, check that your version of Office is not a static version like Office 2019. Go to any desktop Office app, then choose File, then Account. If you're receiving updates automatically, you're all set. If you're not, go to office.com and log in with your education institution account. If you have the option to install Office 365 desktop apps, we recommend it (but you should check with your IT department first if you're using a school-issued device). You can also download free copies of Office on your personal PC at home.

PowerPoint allows presenters to insert video and audio, but did you know that you can record your own voice to narrate your slides? Set your timings and record your narration, and you have an auto-paced slideshow (hello, flipped learning). Screen Recording is often overlooked, perhaps because a lot of people don't know about it, but it is a powerful teaching tool. You can record your screen with any related audio without purchasing costly alternatives. It's built into

PowerPoint. If you're a fan of flipped learning, this is one you must explore. Check the Recording ribbon for this feature.

PowerPoint Recording is available by default in the latest version of Office for PC. If you don't see the Recording ribbon, check your version in File > Info or your ribbon display options in File > Options.

You can also insert 3D models. This is absolutely amazing, especially when you create a PowerPoint and then share it with your students so they can move through the slides on their own. They can turn the objects 360 degrees or zoom in close to notice things they hadn't seen before. (Keep in mind that this is a great solution for kids who want to work with 3D but don't have a 3D printer on hand. They can export their 3D creations from Paint 3D or Minecraft, then insert them into PowerPoint to interact with them and share them with others.)

Insert 3D models in PowerPoint using the Insert ribbon, then choose 3D Models and From Online Sources.

When kids (and adults) discover the myriad new design options available, they tend to get a little too excited about possibilities and often over-design. This can result in messy, distracting, and time-consuming designs that take away from the overall message instead of helping support it.

PowerPoint Designer is one of the tools that helps streamline and strengthen this process. The simple Design Ideas pane helps users choose templates based on an overall theme for their presentation. It's available in PowerPoint desktop or PowerPoint Online, and it works on images, SmartArt, titles, text, bulleted lists, and more. Design Ideas will use artificial intelligence to review your presentation content and select graphics, colors, and features to match. Choose the Design ribbon and then Design Ideas to try it out with some existing slides and introduce it to your students.

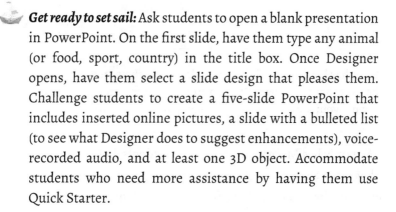 ***Get ready to set sail:*** Ask students to open a blank presentation in PowerPoint. On the first slide, have them type any animal (or food, sport, country) in the title box. Once Designer opens, have them select a slide design that pleases them. Challenge students to create a five-slide PowerPoint that includes inserted online pictures, a slide with a bulleted list (to see what Designer does to suggest enhancements), voice-recorded audio, and at least one 3D object. Accommodate students who need more assistance by having them use Quick Starter.

We simply can't talk about PowerPoint and creativity without telling you about Marija Petreska, an English teacher from Skopje, North Macedonia. She is known throughout the Microsoft community, but everyone agrees that her most magnificent talent is how she taught herself to design in PowerPoint. For anyone who loves aesthetics and is drawn to strong graphics, Marija's skills will amaze you. What's more, she is more than willing to teach all of us her magic.

Marija realized that PowerPoint could be a canvas on which to create art. She began manipulating shapes, colors, and shading to create her own infographics until she had reached such a level of mastery that she now creates all of her own handmade clip art and even background paper in PowerPoint. It's difficult to write about this without showing you how she goes about creating her gorgeous designs:

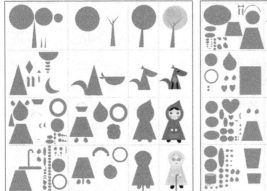 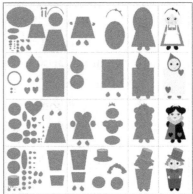

Marija has kindly shared these templates that show step-by-step how she uses shapes in PowerPoint to create stunning graphics. Imagine what your students can design using these as a starting point!

Not only has Marija taught her own students, but she generously teaches others how to create. She formed a PowerPoint Club for students, and she has done (and will do!) live virtual demonstrations with classrooms around the world who want to learn. She has even created an entire in-depth, self-paced course about how to utilize all of this creativity and so much more to organize and deploy a OneNote Class Notebook. The course was offered once online and took about six weeks to complete, but Marija has found a sponsor to make it available online for all of us. She cleverly built the entire course in a OneNote Notebook, so you can learn everything from the basics of setting up a OneNote Notebook to creating stunning **W** and engaging graphic-enhanced pages like Marija does.

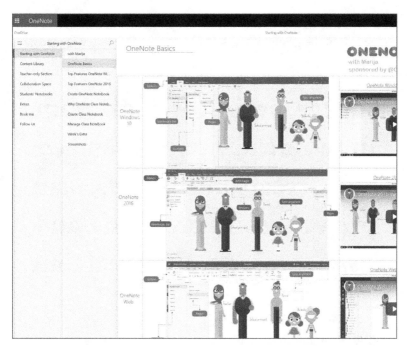

Marija's OneNote course is available broadly for anyone to try.

The Blank Slate: Creating Using Whiteboard

If you haven't yet explored Microsoft's Whiteboard, we sure hope you do after reading this. It is an incredibly diverse and multifaceted tool for collaborative creation. It is just what it sounds like—a whiteboard—but it is an infinite interactive canvas that allows users to share that space with anyone else in the world. Open Whiteboard with your whole class, or open several with small groups in your class. Connect with each other, or connect with others remotely. Once you're in that virtual space, it's time to start creating—engage, brainstorm, diagram, draw, include photos, embed links, create mind maps, plan projects, solve problems, and design projects, all in real time. Whiteboard has an auto-save feature so that, whenever anyone contributes, their work appears live and is saved in the cloud so the rest of the group or class can see it whenever they're ready.

Engage, brainstorm, diagram, draw, include photos, embed links, create mind maps, plan projects, solve problems, and design projects, all in real time.

The team at Whiteboard has worked hard to make sure all of the features we need to create in a classroom are there for us in an easy-to-use way. With one click, you can change the background to a variety of colors (from pastels to black) for design purposes or simply for better readability. Having virtual sticky notes to add to the board makes creative brainstorming a breeze—even if it's with a class across the world. It's fun to experiment with the different inks, line thicknesses, and stickers to enhance the creative process. We love that it can convert handwriting to more readable text to ultimately make a more professional-looking creation, and it also includes the Immersive Reader so all the text on your Whiteboard is accessible to all learners. There are even various backgrounds, like lined papers or grids, that support creativity in math. Teachers or students can use it to poll other members of the Whiteboard and collect responses in real time. Of course, any Whiteboard is super easy to share or export with the click of a button—you can even export it to your OneNote or Teams.

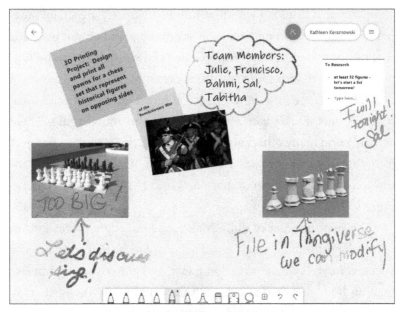

Microsoft Whiteboard is so easy to access inside Windows 10.
Search for "Whiteboard" to find it. It is a fabulous open canvas
on which group members can collaborate in many ways.

Students and teachers love the absolute versatility of Whiteboard as an outstanding collaborative creative tool. The example here shows posted notes, handwritten annotation in digital ink, a colorful background, and the creative toolbar. All team members can view and edit in Whiteboard using the many included digital options.

Let's Play: Creating Using MakeCode

One of the best ways to involve students in creation is to give them a medium that matters. Whether it's art, music, writing, manufacturing, engineering, or baking, people naturally gravitate toward creation-specific contexts. We love being able to combine a digital coding environment with the physical world. Students' eyes positively light up when they see their coding efforts impacting a physical device. Micro:bit is a great way to introduce students to computational thinking with physical devices. They are small, inexpensive, easy to use, and have a variety of input and output methods that can be coded through MakeCode (and which can also be toggled to JavaScript for more advanced learning).

We've worked with students to build makerspace projects like magic wands, rock/paper/scissors games, and mood radio. These activities and many others are easy to find on the MakeCode project website and give educators a quick introduction to hands-on coding activities with students that don't stop at the edge of the computer screen.

The first time Becky did a MakeCode project with her kids at home, they chose the magic wand activity. She hauled out paint stir sticks, colored tape, construction paper, and glitter glue, and in less than an hour they had wands with flashing hearts. The next rainy day, her son asked if he could do some more coding. "What do you want to build?" she asked. "Nothing," he responded. "I just want to work on the project from last week." It turned out he'd been thinking all week long about how to change the code to the wand. Instead of a flashing heart, he got creative and programmed letters to spell his name.

There are many tutorials available at MakeCode.com for
a variety of physical computing devices. Take your pick.

While creating wands is fun, some teachers have taken creation with MakeCode to an entirely different level. Pauline Maas, an Information and Communication Technology (ICT) teacher at Visio School in Amsterdam, Netherlands, works with teen students who are blind or have very low vision. Pauline chooses to use MakeCode with her students because of the highly accessible environment. Other block-based coding tools may simplify learning to code, but they don't have a component that can be interpreted by screen readers or added to by braille keyboards. By using the scripting side of MakeCode, her students can use the tool most effectively. Her students also need a variety of outputs that aren't necessarily visual, so it's important to use physical devices that incorporate music tones. She plugs the micro:bits into external sound devices if needed to amplify the sound in the classroom.

Several of the project ideas Pauline's students have created contribute to their own well-being. One coding project used micro:bit radio signals to allow students to personally identify when a friend came near. Because micro:bit signals are unique, the student coded the devices to output a specific tone for a certain device coming within range. Another project allowed students to hear if their school bag was being moved by programming a motion alarm into the micro:bit.

Pauline knows that her students have challenges ahead of them in life, but she is empowering them, through creation devices using MakeCode, to make their world a better place rather than waiting for someone else to do it for them. For her students, coding is a pathway to a career and future opportunities they may not have had otherwise. Pauline's goal for her students is to empower them to know that they can make a difference, achieve goals, and solve problems no matter what obstacles they might face. They are creators in the truest sense of the word.

Coding is a pathway to a career and future opportunities they may not have had otherwise.

Educators around the world are championing using MakeCode to create devices. STEMUp Education Foundation representative Prabhath Mannapperuma from Colombo, Sri Lanka, told us about the shift in focus from traditional schoolwork to creative programming in his community. STEMUp wanted to change from studying information technology to a mash-up of learning experiences that allowed students to learn coding using MakeCode and to interact with physical devices. Prabhath found that the students in the cities had started learning coding skills, but the skill set hadn't spread to the rural villages. STEMUp started a hackathon for students, provided teacher training, made support videos, and even found people with the ability to translate the micro:bit website into their native Sinhala and Tamil languages. Prabhath was proud to share that 650 volunteers are now registered to deliver MakeCode content to schools, completely free of charge. He reflects that the biggest advantage for the students in Colombo is that they are "opening their eyes to new opportunities in their world." MakeCode helps students and their families see the value of education and connect their classroom experiences to their futures.

One very popular context in today's generation of learners is games. Game design and game making let students create content for themselves and others to experience. Yet the process of game creation is anything but simple. In her book *Reality Is Broken,* Jane

McGonigal outlines dozens of games—many of them rather simplistic—that she and her teammates have created. She contends at the end of her book that "[g]ames aren't leading us to the downfall of human civilization. They're leading us to its reinvention." People have been playing games since the Dark Ages, and their complexity has changed over time. When students become creators of games, they amplify their imaginations, an intrinsic part of our humanity.

Steve Isaacs, a teacher of game design and development at William Annin Middle School and Ridge High School in Basking Ridge, New Jersey, USA, has a succinct goal for his classes. "Everything I do with kids has them as the content creators," he told us. The beauty of game design is that it can be either digital or unplugged. Students can create board games or card games as well as digital games on computers. In Steve's case, his students are often working in MakeCode.

Steve starts his students in MakeCode because he says it's a gateway to learn the important elements of game design while creating fairly simple games, which gives it a low floor but a high ceiling—meaning that kids can get started quickly and without much effort but can do all sorts of creative, limitless learning. He teaches students about designing games that build player confidence but get more challenging, growing with the player's ability. This is easy to point out in MakeCode, where simply changing the frequency an enemy appears, for example, can drastically alter the difficulty of a game. In the micro:bit version of the game Flappy Bird, students press buttons to help the sprite avoid the obstacles. Changing the number and frequency of obstacles makes the game more difficult or even impossible. That brings up another teaching point: playability.

A well-designed game should be the right challenge level so kids don't immediately quit, but instead want to play again and again, whether they win *or* lose. These types of games allow students to play again to beat their own score, play additional levels, or get further in the game.

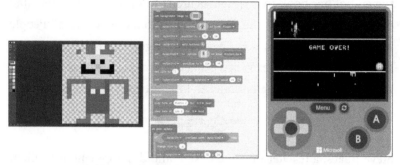

It's a simple equation with MakeCode Arcade: build a sprite, code the game, and play. Image credits to Trevor, a student from Mr. Isaacs's class.

Going beyond Games: Creating Using Minecraft

Steve's favorite game design tool, however, is Minecraft. It was the first tool he used in which students could collaborate, communicate their needs, work in flexible teams, and use content tools together. "You'd think it would complicate things," he commented to us during our interview, "but it actually brings magic into the classroom." His students have options to choose the aesthetics of the game environment within Minecraft, unlimited building supplies, and advanced mechanics that aren't available in a simple coding platform. But Minecraft integrates coding, command blocks, and redstone (basically a powered resource that creates circuit-like connections between elements). Steve states that people are often surprised at the level of complexity that goes into his middle-school students' games. Massive world builds, complicated circuit systems, cause-and-effect situations, and all sorts of creative student-built solutions are easy to spot in his students' work.

Because he believes that all students should have the opportunity to create games, Steve worked with his school's computer science curriculum team to ensure that game design was included in every seventh-grade student's required course work. Because all students now take game design, more girls have signed up for continued coursework in the advanced elective (optional) class, as well as students who didn't have any prior experience in or affinity to gaming. Many students enjoy the class because of its open-ended, project-based learning style. "It allows us to cast a very wide net," Steve explained, "because all types of students can be successful as they choose what to pursue through the learning process."

What's important here is how students immerse themselves in the creative process. One of the best things about the way Steve structures his class is that he helps his students learn that the creative process is not linear. Much like teachers communicate the writing process to their students, Steve shows students how the feedback and revision cycle is important, allowing students to devise solutions to issues brought to their attention by game reviewers.

Each student submits his or her game to a shared drive (like a Class Teams Files space) so the other students can download the game. The students complete a feedback form created by the game designer so the designer can track the feedback and follow up with problems or bugs. One activity asks the game designer to stand behind the game reviewer and watch while they play—without commenting or helping! These structures allow the game designer to see what could be improved and how a new audience would approach the game. In the postgame review debrief, Steve reminds his students that the goal is for the final game to be better for everyone who plays. Sometimes that means thinking about solutions differently or creating entirely new game elements.

When you think about it, students can use a game to demonstrate their understanding of a concept. Phygital Labs, a game-based learning content provider where Becky is a director, has a Minecraft **W** resource pack designed around elementary math concepts. From learning patterns to understanding coordinate grids, students are fighting to gain access to an antidote to a zombie outbreak that is threatening their society. Within the game, students must solve challenges using their math skills. Students can use this same approach to create their own content-review games in any content area. Game-based learning isn't just about engaging students in fun, although it certainly does that. It's also about practicing and building thinking skills that will help students prepare for successful futures.

Another amazing example of students creating in Minecraft comes from Stéphane Cloatre, a technology and robotics teacher at Collège Jeanne d'Arc in Fougères, France. His middle-level students benefited greatly from his focus on developing them as creators. Stéphane began using Minecraft after his students helped him discover it, and he realized the potential to bring more meaningful experiences to his students. He had planned a hands-on learning unit about local history and asked his students to draw blueprints and buildings from the past. He realized how much more powerful it would be for students to create the city in Minecraft, so that's what they did.

In partnership with the local heritage association, Stéphane's students got access to historical documents so they could research what the town looked like in the past. Then, inside Minecraft, students created a version of their city that no longer existed. They started small: one school, one church. Soon they had several models of pieces of the city from the Middle Ages, as students created an environment to merge their research with their creativity. With 120 students working on the project, they got a lot done in a relatively short amount of time. While some students weren't initially comfortable using Minecraft to create, they collaborated with their peers and were soon immersed in the learning experience to the point that frustrations were greatly reduced. In fact, Stéphane found out that some students were pretending to have homework so they would have to work on their Minecraft project at home! Parents commented to Stéphane that their children were more excited to attend school. Local authorities were proud of the students for investing in their own local history. Community members were pleased to hear students describing what once was to their families as they walked around town, with comments like, "I've built that! You should see what it used to look like long ago."

Can you believe this was built in Minecraft? This is
one part of Stéphane's student-built project.

The project was such a success that now Stéphane is leading another project with his students—this time, in the future. Students are creating models of a sustainable version of sections of their own city—one that will solve their own problems and function thirty years in the future. Students will present their solutions to the province authorities. This authentic audience and purpose change the way his students create. Instead of creating an artifact with the teacher in mind, they are creating with a decision-maker in mind. Applying the appropriate audience and purpose to these creation projects changes the way students engage and brings creative juices out of dark corners where they've been lying in wait for a reason to come alive.

Indeed, Minecraft can be leveraged to create virtual prototypes before they are built. Rachel Chisnall, a science teacher at Taieri College outside Dunedin, New Zealand, gave us some great examples of this. She's had students build windmills to study energy—first in Minecraft and then with wooden craft sticks and glue. The students built their models in Minecraft and then refined their prototypes with real materials. When her students couldn't get the windmill to turn the motor in real life (one of the objectives of the build), she talked to the students about the acronym FAIL. In her class, FAIL stands for "first attempt in learning." This mantra guides her students to be design thinkers: to try, test, redesign, hypothesize, align, predict, and start all over again.

Instead of creating an artifact with the teacher in mind, they are creating with a decision-maker in mind.

One of the most remarkable ways to use Minecraft is as a blank slate. The creative mode of Minecraft: Education Edition is much loved by its players because with unlimited resources come unlimited possibilities. One such opportunity arose after Becky's daughter overheard a conversation on one of Becky's planning calls for a project with, Phygital Labs. One of the world builders stated that he was going to "start with a blank world." The builder meant that he would start with an unaltered world in Minecraft, one that was infinite (not a flat world) and hadn't been changed already. Becky's daughter heard "blank world" and asked an important question: "Does he really mean completely blank? Is that possible?" The idea stuck with her. She thought it would be fun to start in a completely empty Minecraft world with just one block. In this scenario, users "spawn" (join the world) on the block and then, in creative mode, start building from the unlimited inventory of materials. The world builder provided her with a Void World, and Becky's daughter loved it. She has been working on the world for months now, building buildings, pathways, gardens, a library, and more. It's a whole village, built entirely from her mind, with no constraints like preexisting topography or features. She loves the open-ended nature of the world and the fact that nothing gets in the way of her vision.

Solving the Puzzle: Creating Using OneNote

All this talk of creative building can make it sound like creativity leaves behind the nuts-and-bolts experience of practical learning. But Microsoft Education tools can be creatively used to help with even something as basic as taking notes. Gloria Enrique is a teacher doing incredible work. Originally from Spain, Gloria now enjoys her career as a teacher of Spanish and ICT at an all-girls Catholic school called Sacred Heart School in Tullamore, Ireland, working with students between the ages of twelve and eighteen. Gloria always thinks and plans around her students' needs and interests first. To do that, she places a high importance on building relationships with them and fostering opportunities. We are so impressed with the way Gloria uses and designs OneNote Notebooks, so we asked her to describe her creation process. Our interview led to inspiring stories of how she creates teamwork exercises in OneNote Notebooks with something called Breakouts. What's more, her creativity inspires her students' creativity, as you'll read in her story below.

To create or organize a OneNote Notebook, the first thing I think about is my students. I focus on what they would like to see there, and how they can learn. Then I plan the activities and start to put the things I think they would like into OneNote. Sometimes I've learned that inserting a table makes it easier for them to write or record. Sometimes when I insert a picture, I have to remember to right-click on it and set it as the background so it will not move when the students are on the page. I try to put myself in the students' place. Right now, so many of them are into unicorns and llamas, so I try to add in lots of unicorns and llamas! I know that as they get older, it will be other things like music videos, but it's always about planning engaging pages with the students in mind. Knowing your students is key for creation.

Knowing your students is key for creation.

Next, I focus on the objective. When I need to teach things like grammar, I know it's important to learn it exactly, but I also have to hold their interest. I think about how they can learn grammar in a different way. They can create a little game on a page and then share it with the rest of the class. They can always use OneNote to record themselves saying something, or they can create a video to insert in there. They can record themselves on Flipgrid and embed it into OneNote. I can make a simple template and then make it attractive in different ways by changing the page color or adding in pictures, different fonts, tables, stickers, audio clips, videos, and activities. It's not just one thing, so I love OneNote for that reason.

There are twenty-five students in my Spanish class. I cannot listen to everyone. With OneNote, it's so easy. They can insert audio right on a OneNote page, and they can even insert video if they want. We used Flipgrid the other day, and they used Spanish to tell me about their dogs, their pets, or even their teddy bears. I learn more about my students, and it's nice.

I believe in creating fun learning opportunities. I created a OneNote Breakout in my ICT classes, just to show the students how to use the different features of OneNote. Here's how I do it. To create a Breakout in OneNote, I start with the first section in the beginning and put a made-up story about why they're trying to escape. On that page, I usually put a bit about how it works, and explain that the students have to pass the different challenges in each section to unlock it to get to the next one. I set a password for each section, then lock that section with a right-click on the section tab to trigger password protection. The students have to solve riddles or a series of questions to arrive at an answer (a word or a set of numbers) that is the password. I do a very easy challenge for the first one to just show them how to do it. On the next page, in my business classes, it's all calculations, so they may have to get a number to get into the next locked section. That can be the password for that section. For Spanish, the clues are often Spanish words. For business, I focus on the content I am teaching. I may put a question about savings, or calculating how much someone has earned, or something like that. I usually have a bit of sweets or something like that to give all of my students as a reward for unlocking all of the sections.

This is the coolest part. In our school, we do a Safe Internet Day, and we created a committee for the kids to learn and share about internet safety. One of the groups created their own OneNote Breakout for other students to learn how to be safe online. I was so surprised when I saw it! It was fantastic! Students enjoyed it so much. I kept hearing, "Oooh, we figured this out! We know the clue! We unlocked the next section!" They were so excited to learn! And the students who made it were proud to have created a learning experience for our entire classroom community. Soon, I had many creators in my classes. By expanding on my little Breakout activity, my students were inspired to create graphically and digitally, and they go far beyond what I could have dreamed of. Creativity is contagious.

Gloria was kind enough to share the actual OneNote Breakout that she used with her students. It is called "Escape the Internet."

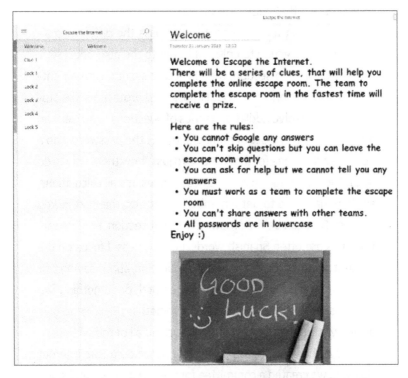

This is the introductory page in Gloria's "Escape the Internet" breakout activity, created in a OneNote Notebook. The sections are locked by being password-protected, and students must solve problems and find answers to unlock each sequential section.

Conclusion

Gloria shows us the power of creating classroom communities by using a rich variety of Microsoft tools and features. Her students have ways to communicate, collaborate, create, think critically, and even think computationally in her ICT classes. Giving her students so many ways to interact and express themselves has built relationships and trust. Gloria is empowering her students with so many skills they will need for the rest of their lives, no matter what careers they choose. Her students feel safe to share and free to be open, and they have spaces to think and create.

Our sincerest hope is that after finishing this chapter, you can't wait to expose your students to new ideas and opportunities to create. All of the educators featured in the Creativity chapter agree that it's critical to purposefully incorporate creation experiences when planning units of learning. Whether you provide scaffolded templates or completely open-ended freedom, we know that, if we are to help our students become their best future selves, we need to move them from being consumers to being creators. Like Gloria with her OneNote examples, that may involve really building relationships with students first and understanding what they want. Like Marija, your journey will hopefully involve some play and experimentation. Like Steve, you may find students have more expertise than you do on certain elements of the tools you're using. Stepping out of your comfort zone is a brave and adventurous thing—and it's also the best thing you can do to truly unleash the creative minds in your classroom.

Creation Anchor Points

⚓ Be mindful and purposeful about incorporating creation opportunities into lessons by choosing the best Microsoft Education tool to accomplish your goals.

⚓ When you plan activities or times for your students to create, it can be scaffolded with frameworks or templates, or it can be incredibly open-ended. Think about which type of lesson works best for you and the students you teach.

⚓ It's fine if your students are more familiar with a tool than you are. You don't have to be an expert; just open the door. Your expertise comes with respect to making sure these creation opportunities align with your curricular goals and objectives.

Crew Member Spotlight:
Stéphane Cloatre

Watch and listen as Stéphane Cloatre from France tells us about his students' experiences as creators.

Use your Flipgrid app to scan the QR code for an augmented reality experience or use any QR code reader to view as a standard video. You can also access the link to this video from the Wakelet collection for this chapter.

CRITICAL AND COMPUTATIONAL THINKERS

According to the National Council for Excellence in Critical Thinking, the range of cognitive processes involved in critical thinking is enormous. They define critical thinking as "conceptualizing, applying, analyzing, synthesizing, and/or evaluating information gathered from, or generated by, observation, experience, reflection, reasoning, or communication, as a guide to belief and action." That's a lot of verbs! Critical thinking is more than the levels of Bloom's Taxonomy, more than Depth of Knowledge Level 4, and more than can be simply assessed on a rubric. After all, educators are charged with preparing students for a world that does not yet exist. We can only hope that the thinking skills we help our students develop will best prepare them for their futures.

We have a range of technology tools that can help facilitate deeper levels of thinking. After all, it's not about the tools themselves. The products, software, and apps are simply a means to get the thinking to appear. When we ask students to conceptualize, they need a place to sketch, and digital ink becomes critical. When we ask students to analyze information, it's helpful to visualize the data with Microsoft Excel. When we ask students to synthesize their learning, they can choose to build a model in Minecraft. Thinking critically—and computationally—isn't done in isolation from technology; it's done best with the tools necessary to showcase this thinking. At its finest, technology serves to amplify learning.

One Tool to Rule Them All: Critical Thinking Using OneNote

There are a lot of edtech tools in the world, and many of them do specific things very well. We might use one tool for brainstorming, another for drafting, another for note-taking, and yet another for annotating. While it's true that we should choose the best tool for each task, it's also true that students (and teachers!) need an anchor point. There should be one place where students can return to do much of their thinking and planning, and one place where they can return to get information they need provided by their teacher. Having too many places to go for these basic components of classroom life confuses many learners and provides one more hoop for struggling students. That's why OneNote is the perfect Swiss Army Knife of education tools.

Before we go any further in this chapter, we really want you to see what critical thinking could look like using OneNote. We want you to have a visual reference of what skills can be incorporated to bring students through the various stages of Bloom's Taxonomy. As you read through the examples in the chart, think about ways you could adapt these ideas to create critical thinking lessons for your specific age group or subject. Knowing what that might look like will help set the stage for some of the other critical thinking examples we will share in this chapter.

Knowledge

- Teachers share a template page with questions about a science article to give students background before completing an in-class lab assignment.

- Students find a historical map of a place they are studying in geography and label the map with modern place names.

- Students keep a vocabulary word journal of new words they learn while reading. Students create a tagging system to categorize words in the text inside their notes.

- Teachers share math problems with students to complete. Students show their work in the Notebook and leave one audio example explaining how they solved a problem for the teacher to review.

Comprehension

- Teachers share a page with an embedded video from YouTube. Students write a summary of the main points of the video.

- Students create an outline of an article about a current event.

- Students describe how they would change something about their school.

- Students put the steps to solve a math problem in the appropriate order, then demonstrate how to use the steps. The teacher watches Ink Replay to see the student work in action.

Application

- Students read an article that has been sent to OneNote from an online source and draw conclusions based on the text. Students annotate the article in digital ink.

- Teachers share a page of analogies with students to solve away from school.

- Students brainstorm why a historical event was an important turning point in a conflict by co-completing a graphic organizer in the Collaboration space of a Class Notebook.

- Students determine how different athletic skills are related through reviewing the basic movements and muscle groups utilized. Students add images from online sources, text, and digital ink to show their thinking.

Analysis

- Teachers share a page with an embedded Sway showing multiple forms of art in the same time period. Students write a reflection comparing the pieces at the bottom of the page in OneNote.

- Students dissect a piece of code to look for bugs. The code is embedded on the OneNote page from MakeCode.com, and the students screen-clip pieces and write their analysis in a chart on the page.

- Teachers ask students to find evidence to support an opinion for an essay. Students must find evidence and cite sources in an organized structure in a Wakelet collection. Students add their Wakelet collections to a page in the Collaboration space so they can be viewed by other students.

- Students study fractions using favorite recipes from home. Using Office Lens, students capture the recipe and send it to a OneNote page. They then double, triple, and halve the recipe and write new directions and ingredient lists for those scales.

Synthesis

- Teachers share a set of primary sources to the Content Library for students to review. Students work in small teams to predict which event in history these primary sources reference, then write their conclusion in the Collaboration space in their group section.

- Students share their personal narratives by pasting them into the Collaboration space for others to review. Students suggest revisions to each other's writing inside the page.

- Students create a sketchnote based on a video embedded on the OneNote page using digital ink.

- Students invent a new way to reward good behavior at school. Students work in teams inside OneNote's group Collaboration space and share a copy of their final recommendation to their Class Team.

Evaluation

- Teachers share a link to an article about a controversial issue to the OneNote Content Library. Students read the article and then answer questions from an embedded Form about their opinion after reading the article. Students review the class responses and write a justification of their own opinions in their Private Notebooks.

- Students select award-winning children's books to read to younger students. Students make a class list in the Collaboration space so they will not duplicate books. Students record their reviews in Flipgrid and then embed them on a OneNote page of a new shared Notebook, adding a summary of the book at the top of the page. Students publish a link to this shared Notebook to the school website, so younger learners can listen to books being read at home by older students simply by visiting the school website and accessing OneNote Online.

- Students create their own rubrics for meeting grade-level standards using tables in OneNote. The teacher gathers these rubrics and adds samples to the Content Library for students to revise their own based on peer-created examples.

- Students create a marketing portfolio for their choice of consumer product that utilizes OneNote as the organizational structure.

People who have interacted with Becky in professional development sessions or conferences have likely heard her say that OneNote is her favorite app of all time. She first started using OneNote early on as a professional tool. When she was hired as part of a three-person team to launch a proof-of-concept 1:1 program for ninety middle school students in Kent School District, Washington, USA, the teacher team began using a shared Notebook to do their team planning. They noticed right away how flexible the tool was for brainstorming, collaborating, and information gathering. They were really impressed with the ability they had to work offline and then sync up once they returned to campus. It was highly effective as a professional tool, and when the school opened in the fall of 2005, they started using OneNote with the students. It was perfect for annotating text in language arts, marking up maps and images in social studies, writing out solutions in math, and diagramming in science.

Its infinite canvas makes for a flexible workspace, and its structure is natively comfortable in education: pages, sections, and notebooks.

The students quickly came to depend on OneNote. It was where they did all their work, especially collaborative work. In the project-based environment, shared workspaces were necessary. The students became incredibly proficient at using OneNote, and anytime they started a new unit, teachers would hear students all around the room gathering in their work teams say, "Who's making the Notebook to share?" The ability to work, think, and plan together was essential to them.

These students taught each other a lot about using OneNote effectively. (Want to get better at an edtech tool? Use it with your students.) One group of students had used tags to place colored squares throughout the lists of tasks they had created for their group as they planned their project work. They had assigned a colored tag to each group member, and they could use the Find Tags feature to generate their own to-do lists, which were sorted automatically by tag. The self-regulation and critical thinking taking place was noteworthy, and the tool allowed them to be more efficient workers.

Often, students would share their Notebooks with their teachers as well. Seeing students' thinking in real time, often in their own writing via digital ink, is priceless. In fact, Dana Piehl, a science teacher for Kent School District, gets credit for being one of the teachers who identified the need for Microsoft to incorporate real-time OneNote syncing for students. With ninety OneNote Notebooks open and syncing students' science work in real time, she nearly broke the server! Subsequently, Robert Baker, director of technology at Cincinnati Country Day School in Cincinnati, Ohio, USA, worked tirelessly with the OneNote team to make Dana's dream a reality by launching Class Notebook.

More than one of Becky's past students have returned to tell her how thankful they were to have learned OneNote in middle school, and one commented that it, *more than any other tool,* helped her be successful in college. But our favorite OneNote story comes from a student whom we'll call Peter.

Peter struggled in elementary school. He was disorganized, struggled with executive function skills, and took a long time to complete tasks. He had a low reading level and often felt he couldn't contribute to a group project like the other students. Peter had an individualized education program that granted him extra time to complete assignments as well as some other accommodations, but he hadn't been able to see his own value in the classroom for a long time. Peter was doing about average-level work in Becky's seventh-grade humanities class. Throughout the year, Becky saw him become more willing to share his thoughts and participate more actively in his group projects. She made sure he had access to leveled text so he could discuss the same concepts as the rest of his group and additional time to prepare for class discussions. Becky was still surprised when Peter volunteered to share about his year in the school program at the spring family night, which would be attended by more than a hundred families who would hear all about what the students had been up to for the past year. Peter missed the preparation meeting Becky had with all of the student presenters, and, as you might imagine, she was more than a little nervous to let an unprepared, unrehearsed student get up in front of an audience and share something she hadn't even heard yet. But Peter told her that he'd practiced at home and that he was ready, so she said he could participate. When Peter's turn came at the spring family night, he moved forward, took the microphone, and spoke clearly. Becky will never forget his first words: "I used to not be a very good student. But OneNote changed my life."

Peter went on to describe how he now had access to his team projects from home and how he could use that extra time to work outside of class instead of being locked into the timeline of a six-period day at school. He shared how this additional access allowed him to feel that he added value to his team as a contributor and how his classmates showed their appreciation for the work he'd done outside of the school day. He talked about how he could always find what he needed because of the search function, when before he had struggled to bring the right assignment home to work on. He shared how he hadn't lost an assignment the entire year because of OneNote, and how he'd been able to use the inking tools to help his brain better understand long pieces of text. No one can be sure if Becky's face portrayed the emotion she felt when he was done, but she couldn't have been prouder of Peter for sharing. He showed everyone, in his twelve-year-old-boy words, how a tool can remove obstacles and support success in ways not previously done.

"I used to not be a very good student. But OneNote changed my life."

Many students need this kind of support to be successful, and often students struggle with these skills more than the content of their classes. OneNote's flexible nature, anytime access, mobile-ready interface, and always-on technology allow students to jot notes and work on projects in the moment. Executive function incorporates skills such as organizing, planning, prioritizing, and self-monitoring. OneNote's Notebook structure, with sections and pages set up like a physical three-ring binder, helps students stay organized like no other tool we've ever seen.

With the addition of Class Notebook functionality, teachers can share pages with students as assignments, view student work in real time, leave feedback in multiple forms, and engage in whole group collaboration. It's critical thinking at a whole new level.

One of our examples of this comes from a language arts teacher using OneNote. Kelli Etheredge, currently the Teaching and Learning Resources Director at St. Paul's Episcopal School in Mobile, Alabama, USA, teaches *The Count of Monte Cristo* in ways that lead students to use OneNote to organize their thinking in a new and innovative manner. She gives each student a copy of the OneNote Notebook to start, and then each student writes their own notes, makes their own changes, and marks up text throughout the Notebook.

Starting midway through the book, Kelli pivots and assigns students a role in the upcoming "trial" of the Count of Monte Cristo. Students now have to read with fresh purpose: to determine what can be included as evidence to support their role or side in the trial. They also have to go back through their notes to see what else can be used. The students are now even more highly motivated to pay attention to details in the text as everything is potential evidence for the future trial. The prosecution must determine which charges to bring against the count, which means learning about local laws and penalties first. After the trial is over, students write an essay answering the prompt, "Is Dante really the hand of God?" Kelli reports that many students change their initial views about the count following the trial, a sign of great critical thinking and reflection.

But as Kelli is quick to point out, an assignment like this would be nearly impossible to pull off without the right organizational tool. All of this content can be organized in one Class Notebook, and the incredible amount of information gathered is stored in one place where students have access to the thoughts and ideas of everyone on their team. "For my students, staying connected to each other for school work is like having a phone and an internet connection," she explained to us. "Kids expect to have the ability to collaborate." Students use OneNote to share resources, task lists, conversations, and much more. The use of OneNote is so ubiquitous that the older students she works with aren't surprised by the ease of access like students years ago might have been.

One of the highlights of using OneNote for this class is the integration of Office Lens, a free app for any mobile device. Kelli's students can often be seen sketching, designing, planning, and brainstorming on physical whiteboards around the room. Students then capture these think sessions with Office Lens by snapping a photo. Office Lens doesn't just capture a photo, however. It adjusts for skew, allows for cropping, and renders text with optical character recognition so that the text within the image is searchable when sent to OneNote via the in-app menu. When technology can enhance the critical thinking process (instead of getting in the way), students benefit. When physical work can be accessed, archived, and searched digitally later, purposeful connections can be made. Office Lens brings a new level of access to students, as it can capture book pages, posters, handouts, presentations, images, and more.

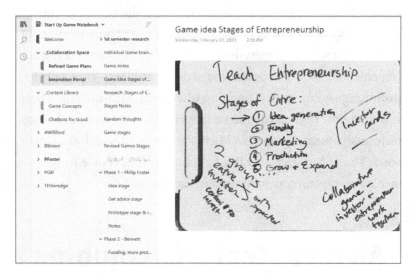

Here's an example of one of Kelli's student's captures—brainstormed
on a physical whiteboard and then scanned to OneNote with Office
Lens for safekeeping, searchability, and future brainstorming.

Another feature that supports critical thinking is the ability to work in ink. Plenty of research studies remind us that students learn better when they can write their thoughts. Because we all learn and process in different ways, it is important to allow students to find what works best for them. Rather than requiring typewritten work for all, we can (and should) give students choices to use modalities that enhance their own learning. Many students would undoubtedly choose to handwrite, diagram, highlight, annotate, doodle, draw, sketch, and solve in digital ink. Digital ink is highly effective for many reasons. First, it's clean! Students don't have to scramble for a better eraser, scratch out messy writing, or sharpen a pencil. And we all know that a clean workspace makes for more focused thoughts. Next, digital ink combines all the benefits of digital text with the benefits of handwriting. Digital ink in OneNote is searchable, saved indefinitely and automatically, and colorful. In our experience, a choice of color alone increases the likelihood that a student will enjoy the writing experience. In Microsoft products, we can convert handwriting to text, so once again students can choose to view and access in the way that meets their individual needs. All these features combine to reduce the cognitive load on the student—especially in a world language or math classroom, where students would have been spending time finding equation editors or alternate symbols to complete assignments properly. Microsoft gives us—and students— options to enhance critical thinking by allowing choice in how we take notes, organize, remember, and learn best.

All these features combine to reduce the cognitive load on the student.

To be clear, OneNote's capabilities aren't just well suited for use by teachers in the humanities. Cal Armstrong is a high school (students ages fourteen to eighteen) mathematics teacher at Appleby College, a private school outside Toronto, Ontario, Canada. In OneNote, Cal embeds any necessary elements, like a Forms quiz, YouTube video, or screen capture, for students to reference. They can split-screen their own OneNote pages with the teacher reference materials in the same Notebook. Separate elements like a textbook, physical paper, and electronic devices only separate the elements that support learning, which creates a disconnect in students' brains that Cal hopes to avoid. "It creates a friction they have to fight against," he explained. His students make connections among content pieces and draw connections by layering their work with color and images. Because of OneNote's infinite canvas, student work never has to go to the end of the page. "Our whole world is full of confined spaces," he said. "Why not open up one more door for students?"

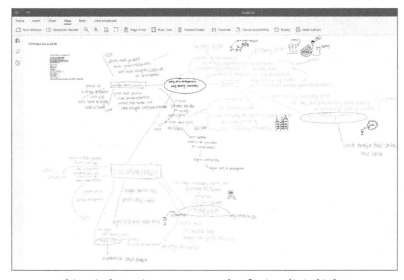

This mind map is a great example of using digital ink to demonstrate thinking in OneNote. OneNote's infinite canvas allows for students to be unconstrained by letter-sized paper.

Get ready to set sail: If you have access to OneNote and a digital inking device (like a mobile device, iPad, or touch screen Windows device), sketch your next brainstorm, plan, design, or note in digital ink. Use your fingers to navigate the space. Use color. You'll be hooked.

Merging OneNote with Augmented Reality: Critical Thinking Using OneNote in Combination with Paint 3D, Merge Cubes, and Teams

Thinking critically involves looking at things in new ways, examining different perspectives, employing various modalities, and synthesizing information. True critical thinking often leads not just to answers but also to more questions and some pretty awesome discussions. It is a thing of beauty to watch a modern-day teacher teach the same concepts we learned in school but in ways that we never would have imagined. One such innovative teacher is Sarah. This feisty teacher from Falkirk, Scotland, works hard to keep her finger on the pulse of the latest technologies. Sarah teaches high school biology, but she cleverly augments her instruction to help students see things in purposeful and relevant ways. As she explains in her story, she innovates by using a combination of Microsoft products and Merge Cubes, which are inexpensive, soft rubber cubes that are designed to be held in the hand. There are raised patterns on each side of the cube that, when scanned with Merge apps, launch engaging augmented reality experiences. Sarah has found a way to "merge" this clever technology with some of our favorite Microsoft tools!

I only use the Merge Cubes when the curriculum allows me to. And that's probably the biggest part. I don't try to force it. I find that it works really well when we study cells. Cells are three-dimensional structures, but whenever students look at one in a book, they're flat. And they don't understand that these are three-dimensional structures. So as soon as you can have something that they can manipulate in their hand, they get that idea—whether it's first years or eighteen-year-old advanced, higher kids. Suddenly they get that it's a three-dimensional structure. They see all the parts inside it.

The first time I used Merge Cubes to study cells, I did it with my oldest pupils. They were seventeen, and they were amazed! They thought it was phenomenal! One of them did say, "Oh, I can see it really big, and I see it's three-dimensional! I can see the back of it." That's one thing I don't think they'd ever actually thought about—what the cell looked like from the outside, around the back. Because they'd never been shown that picture in a textbook. Instead, what they'd always seen was a cross-section, which made the cell appear very flat to them.

With the Merge Cubes, they were able to explore the cell, and they were able to talk about it with each other and with me. But I still had that question, "Well, how do I know they have actually learned it?"

The activity was to look at the cell with the Merge Cube, discuss it, and talk about what each part did, using the other resources that they had—the textbook, the diagrams, and so on. I wanted then to ask, "What is that part in the diagram or in the model, and what does it do?" That's when I needed to assess their learning, so they took screenshots of what they were seeing and put them in OneNote, and then they were able to ink on top of it and label and explain the functions. For my students who didn't have an inkable device, I do have an inkable device, so I set the screenshots of the 3D cells as a background on a OneNote page. Students used their keyboards to add labels to parts they were seeing and just typed descriptions of the functions of each part. That was my assessment of what they had learned from the activity.

They thought it was quite good that it was a picture of the image from the Merge Cube that we'd actually taken and put into OneNote. I love that I can set an assignment like this in OneNote and then just pass it out through Teams, because it keeps everything together. Everything is in each pupil's Notebook, so I can go back through and see what any particular student has done for all of their assignments within OneNote. Of course, they can also go back and see it. I can send them back into their Notebooks to have them revisit that activity anytime.

It may sound really complicated in the beginning, but if you just follow that work flow, it's a lot easier than you'd think!

We are so grateful to Sarah, who is truly a consummate educator W in every way. She wanted everyone to know that this is something anyone can do, so she outlined the steps for us, and you can find them in our book's Wakelet collection.

Get ready to set sail: It's okay to start small when combining multiple apps. Try opening Paint 3D and looking through the library of 3D images. Find one that ties into content you are teaching and place it on the canvas. Click on Menu, then Share, and send it to OneNote. Then distribute that page to your students using OneNote Class Notebook. If you are feeling extra ambitious, we have included all of Sarah's directions in our Wakelet collection for this book, and you can hear from Sarah directly if you scan the Flipgrid QR code at the end of this chapter.

Opening Access to More Learners: Critical Thinking Using Immersive Reader

It's generally accepted that people need to learn to read. Reading grants people access to information, and informed citizens are better citizens. Reading is likely the most core skill in all of education. In his discussion of critical reading as a foundation to critical thinking, Dan Kurland, professor of developmental literacy at the University of Massachusetts and author of *Know What It Says . . . What Does It Mean: Critical Skills for Critical Reading,* states that critical reading is a technique for discovering information and ideas within a text, while critical thinking is a technique for evaluating information and ideas, for deciding what to accept and believe. It seems that critical reading must come before critical thinking. Once students understand text (critical reading), they can evaluate it (critical thinking). But the two powers have a symbiotic relationship. Good readers are constantly monitoring how well they understand the text, and if the claims presented are reliable. This means good readers are thinking critically about reading.

The consequences of not learning how to read effectively are dramatic. Studies show that children who don't have a good grasp of reading between ages seven and twelve are more likely to drop out of school, serve time in a correctional facility, and earn a smaller income as an adult. The list of obstacles a student may have to learning to read is long, and yet teacher preparation in this area is short. Most teacher education programs spend little time on reading challenges such as dyslexia and dysgraphia, and even fewer give general education teachers preparation for working with language learners (in the United States, students whose first language is not English are often identified as *English Language Learners*, or ELL).

There's a reason we're spending time in the critical thinking section of this book on tools that help students read. Access to text is a core part of learning to read, and being able to read is a core part of learning to think critically. We cannot do one without the other.

Access to text is a core part of learning to read, and being able to read is a core part of learning to think critically. We cannot do one without the other.

This is where the learning tools built into many of the Office products truly support student learning in new ways. First among these is Immersive Reader, which offers students help with learning to read. The app was initially designed to assist with the many challenges that a student with dyslexia may have but has been found to reach so many more groups. Students with dysgraphia, students with autism, and students with low vision were among the first to notice the incredible power of the Immersive Reader interface. But it also turns out to be incredibly useful for students who are struggling to read because of such things as a concussion or a broken arm. Students and adults of all reading levels enjoy the read-aloud feature, color themes, and font choices. We can even allow students to capture a photo of a poster, worksheet, or textbook using the Office Lens app. The app has special technology called optical character recognition that converts words in a photo into actual text so it becomes "readable." From within the Office Lens app, anyone can use the built-in Immersive Reader feature to read text aloud from the picture.

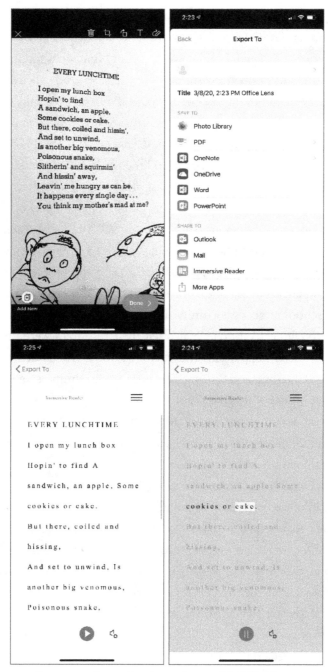

Capture a photo of a piece of text with Office Lens.
Share to Immersive Reader and listen. It's magic!

Having been updated many times since its inception, Immersive Reader now includes translation options for language learners, a picture dictionary to help build vocabulary, and line focus for students whose tracking skills need support. Immersive Reader is available not only throughout the Office suite (and shows off especially well in OneNote) but also in many other web-based and mobile apps such as Flipgrid, Wakelet, Buncee, Nearpod, Canvas, and ThingLink.

Immersive Reader is used around the world to support students in building their thinking strategies. The ease of use that comes with OneNote and Immersive Reader can be a helpful part of allowing students to succeed academically. Michelle Budge, a teacher of English and media studies for school years 9–13 at Taieri College in Dunedin, New Zealand, has a passion for using this tool to boost literacy and engagement. She saw the diversity and literacy challenges at her school as an opportunity to do more for her students (ages twelve to eighteen). Michelle also felt their resources were limited, and she wasn't happy with the current growth her students were making in reading and writing. She began using Immersive Reader with her students to give them an opportunity to have text read aloud, use text and reading preferences, increase grammar awareness, build language skills, and access visuals in new ways through the combined use of Office Lens and OneNote.

Michelle's biggest focus for using Immersive Reader was in the core skill of essay writing, which all her year nine and year ten students are required to do. Two students with special challenges were targeted for increased support through Immersive Reader. Michelle set up a scaffolded lesson plan in which students used Immersive Reader to dictate their responses and, with the Read Aloud function, to check for text structure. She found that her students were motivated to incorporate her feedback when it was given in audio format or included emoji and colorful ink, so that became her feedback delivery method. We just love that Michelle pointedly considered and responded to how her students chose to access feedback to enhance their learning.

One of the major benefits of using Immersive Reader is the ability to personalize the interface for everyone. Color settings, font choices, read-aloud speed, and line-focus options are just a few of the ways students can differentiate their learning experience and access text in new ways. This can be used to anyone's advantage, from struggling readers to proficient readers, young learners to adult readers. Upper-level students studying *Beowulf* may find the Read Aloud feature incredibly helpful, since audio input can greatly increase text comprehension. Adult readers may wish to use larger font size or dark-themed colors to read through long emails using dark mode or to proofread a high-stakes message before sending it. Many of us can benefit from using the Dictate feature to initially get our thoughts out, and then use the Read Aloud feature to play it back so we can find ways to improve it. Because Immersive Reader is built into so many Office products, students know that they have access to these supports beyond their time in school—as adults, business leaders, and community members.

Students know that they have access to these supports beyond their time in school— as adults, business leaders, and community members.

Jennifer Verschoor, head of innovation and technology at St Andrew's Scots School in Buenos Aires, Argentina, led her teachers to Immersive Reader as a solution for students to get the reading support they need. Jennifer has a diverse population of students, so there are several native languages among the students in the school. She feels strongly about equitable access to learning and resources, so she guided St Andrew's Scots School to be the first in Argentina to use Immersive Reader with students.

Her students share iPads at the school, so they simply log into OneNote Online and use Immersive Reader from inside the browser. Jennifer showed other teachers at her school how to snap photos of text with Office Lens and then send it to OneNote for the students to access inside their Class Notebook. "It's a blend of modalities," Jennifer likes to point out. Once that scanned text is in Immersive Reader, students can turn on the translation feature to access and understand the information.

For some of her students, it is the first time they have heard their schoolbooks read aloud in their native Spanish. She also has students speaking Mandarin, Portuguese, French, and English, so the translation features in Immersive Reader are highly valued. She told us the story of one sixteen-year-old student who had struggled with reading his entire life. By using Immersive Reader's tools, he made significant improvements—so much that his mother reported crying when she opened his bedroom door and saw him reading on his bed for the first time in his life.

"The effects are greater than we can even think of," Jennifer told us when we spoke about her experiences. "It's a life-changing experience for students because they can finally find a voice; they become autonomous learners." Isn't that what educating critical thinkers is all about?

Get ready to set sail: Download the Office Lens app to your mobile device. Find a piece of paper, textbook, poster, or worksheet. Snap a photo, then adjust the cropping as needed. Then Export to Immersive Reader and see what happens. You'll need internet access for this process to work.

I Was Just Thinking . . . Critical Thinking Using Flipgrid

From the very beginning, we've known that Flipgrid is a premier product for explaining thinking verbally. Because it's a video-based platform, we can see and hear students' expressions, pauses, and sometimes even circuitous reasoning as they explain how and why they think the way they do. In the first two years after Flipgrid came on the scene, we saw many, many posts on Twitter from educators scrambling to think of ways they could use this in their math classrooms.

This is the perfect time to introduce an educator who focuses on exactly that—having students explain their thinking in a math class. Jen Saarinen was a math teacher at Kickemuit Middle School in the Bristol Warren Regional School District in Bristol, Rhode Island, USA. She taught the same group of sixth and seventh grade students (ages fourteen to eighteen) for two years. Like many math teachers, Jen struggled with finding ways to get her students to verbally express their math thinking. Jen has high expectations for her students, so she also sought ways for her students to be metacognitive in being able to reflect on how they solved a math problem. Additionally, Jen saw value in embracing new technologies that help her students achieve more and master her course content. She saw the value in Flipgrid and decided to give it a try with her students.

W   To accomplish her goal, she eased into using Flipgrid. She talked about it with her students first, let them work in groups (for support and accountability), and chose one specific goal at a time. For instance, one of the first critical thinking objectives she expected of her students was "Perseverance and Understanding Problems." She assigned each group a complex, multistep problem and gave them supports like graphic organizers. Then she gave them time to "huddle up," decide on a solution strategy, and explain their thinking on camera within the Flipgrid app. Purposefully, Jen had set the admin controls to moderate the topic, so no group could see another's response until Jen unlocked the topic and was ready to share all of the videos with the whole group.

Then Jen orchestrated a beautiful segue to her next critical thinking objective, which was "Constructing Viable Arguments and Critiquing the Thinking of Others." Students were able to view and reflect on the video solutions from other groups, and they completed feedback forms that were thoughtful and analytic in nature. Flipgrid allows for video responses to any topic video, so students were also able to verbalize that feedback.

Then Jen blew this lesson wide open by requiring her students to look at responses that had come from all of the other math classes on her team—almost one hundred students! Jen enjoyed seeing how students of varying abilities succeeded in these tasks. Some were precise and analytical in their critical thinking, other students excelled at the art of communicating their understanding, and still others had a talent for providing purposeful and respectful feedback. This class community was collaborating and communicating in a creative way to think critically about math.

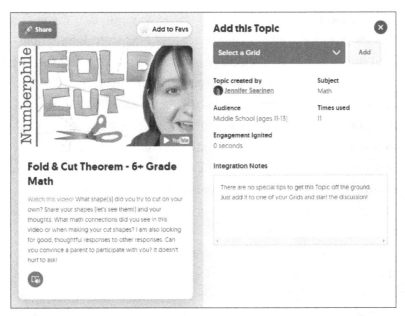

You can find more than forty of Jen's lessons on Flipgrid in the Disco Library within the website, which houses a collection of reusable lessons ready to use with your own students. Just use the filter to search for her name, then select a topic and add her lesson to your own Grid.

Walking a Mile in Another's Shoes: Critical Thinking Using Skype in the Classroom

The innovative and progressive teachers of today are those who are always on a quest to challenge their students not merely to learn the content but also to question it. Doing so requires teaching students the other Cs we've been talking about but also going beyond those Cs to generate an open and accepting attitude that fosters such values as empathy. Achieving those kinds of insights requires very thoughtful and pointed instructional planning. Technologies like those found in the suite of education tools available from Microsoft can help.

Mio Horio is a teacher who is impeccably skilled at doing this kind of purposeful planning. She teaches English to high school–aged students at Shiga Prefectural Maibara Senior High School. The school is in a rural and isolated community in Japan, and Mio's students often feel that they have no use for English—that it is something they will never need or use. Mio knows that it is not enough to just tell the students that it is a requirement; she wants them to really buy into learning to love English and using it in ways that can change their outlook. To get them to practice using the language, Mio crafts brilliant, authentic experiences in which her students use their voices beyond her classroom.

Mio uses Skype in the Classroom to bring English to life for her students by connecting them to communities in more than twenty-five countries. Her students now enjoy communicating in English and learning about global issues and culture by speaking with others from around the world. We can't think of a better example to share than Mio's story of how Skype in the Classroom can be leveraged to craft authentic, problem-based learning opportunities that enable critical thinking on many levels.

First of all, the reason why I started applying technology to my classes stems from the students' low motivation in learning English. Since we live in an area that has few connections to the world, many of my students had no idea why they had to study English but studied it simply because they needed the subject to enter university. When they graduated from high school, they expressed relief at no longer having to study English. So, I started to provide authentic opportunities to communicate in English, connecting my students with those in other countries who could not communicate in our native language.

One good example of this is my English class of third years (students who are seventeen and eighteen years old). We had read a passage in English about the environmental issue of palm oil in Borneo. When we finished reading it, my students debated whether the people in Borneo should create more palm tree plantations to harvest the palm oil. Most of my students sided with preserving the environment and agreed that people in Borneo should not plant palm trees anymore. But then we connected with some Malay students in Borneo via Skype in the Classroom and asked what they thought about these issues. My students discovered that the perspective of Malay students was the total opposite of theirs. They told us that the palm industry is closely connected to their life. If the industry were to stop, lots of people would lose their jobs. They also explained how the loss of palm oil would affect their own life since it is widely used as cooking oil and fuel. By asking further questions and hearing local students' thoughts, my students were able to enrich their own perspective and learn things that weren't written in the textbook.

All my students were surprised and impressed to hear the local perspective from Borneo, even though some of these issues were mentioned in the passage they had read. I believe this is the power of connection. The real connection gives authenticity to what they studied since students can feel and understand the people's concern directly. In other words, the real connection creates empathy, which enables students to take someone's concern as their own. This occurs because they learn through the voices of students in the same generation even though they are in a different country and were raised with different cultural backgrounds.

This kind of connections-based learning—the pedagogical approach created by Sean Robinson—is especially effective for my students, who live in a homogeneous community and mainly rely on mass media for information about the world outside of our area of Japan. Such circumstances can easily lead to bias, but the real connections we make have the potential to break such biases.

Mio is not only challenging her students to think beyond traditional schooling methods, but she also requires them to think beyond their own community. Building bridges between their rural community and the world, her students gain new perspectives and explore global learning in ways that are otherwise impossible. Her students communicate with other students across the world via the Skype in the Classroom platform and are encouraged to learn about the world on their own. By bringing in studies of current events, not only does she boost their communication skills and raise their global awareness, but she also stresses critical thinking to evaluate, synthesize, and innovate. She has taught them to care about their world, and in doing so, they relish opportunities to communicate in English so they can learn enough to make a difference.

Building bridges between their rural community and the world, her students gain new perspectives and explore global learning in ways that are otherwise impossible.

It is no surprise that Mio has won awards for her innovative work: she won the President Award from the Japan International Cooperation Agency, and she has been a finalist for the world-renowned Global Teacher Prize. We are very lucky to have her as a member of our Microsoft community as a Microsoft Innovative Educator Expert and a Skype Master Teacher.

I'll Call My Agent:
Critical Thinking Using Minecraft

Although Minecraft: Education Edition has been around since 2017 it wasn't until recently that Kathi overcame her hesitation and finally took the plunge. Through her work as a professional learning specialist for insight2execution, she was invited to attend a special Minecraft Certified Trainer event for Microsoft's United States–based training partners. The two-day event was hosted by the one and only Meenoo Rami, who was the learning solutions program manager for Minecraft: Education Edition at the time and remains a global champion for great learning experiences for students everywhere.

My first NPC and a
board with a message!

Creating in Minecraft is completely addictive—and you can
capture your progress using the in-game camera and portfolio.

Within a matter of hours, Kathi realized she had nothing to be nervous about. She figured out how to build her first-ever Minecraft house, added a non-player character (NPC), and wrote notes on a board—and she loved it. It's through play that adult learners begin to understand how powerful Minecraft is for developing critical thinking.

On the second day of Kathi's training, Meenoo introduced her to something called the Agent. The Agent is only available in Minecraft: Education Edition and is a character that can be programmed to do tasks. Meenoo explained that the Agent could build an entire house with some simple code. Using MakeCode, anyone can create some code that would direct the Agent to travel in a rectangle while placing blocks, then go up a level and repeat, and continue in this way until the house is complete. Meenoo ran a demonstration of this on the screen in the front of the room, and sure enough, her agent crafted an entire building in seconds as the participants watched in awe.

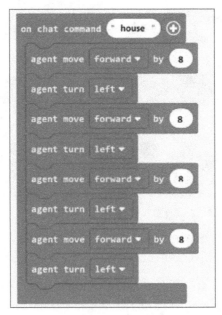

Kathi was so proud of her first piece of Minecraft code!

Because Microsoft MakeCode is integrated into the game, the conference participants were using the same interface students would use to program physical computing devices, but in the digital world. The image here shows Kathi's first effort at coding her Agent to build her house. If you know anything about coding, you can see that what she made was a program where when she typed the word "house" in the Chat, the Agent went forward and made left turns until it had made an 8×8 square.

Of course, Kathi's Agent had just done a lot of walking and hadn't built a thing because she hadn't told it to place any blocks. The sheer beauty of an exercise like this is that it's easy to become addicted to troubleshooting, which is the heart of critical thinking. Kathi "debugged" and revised her code until she got her Agent to do what she wanted. Over the next hour or so, she learned how to adjust those numbers to make the house rectangular, how to get the Agent to place blocks, and how to have her Agent go up one level of blocks to repeat the process, layer by layer. She also learned to use loops to simplify the code so she had fewer blocks to add but her Agent could still complete the build.

Kathi didn't give up until she had accomplished what may seem like a simple construction, but the entire exercise was about exploration, perseverance, grit, determination, being okay with making mistakes, and finding resources that could help her learn. Within an hour, she had a code that built a house that had three stories . . . and she had exemplified what critical thinking is all about.

As both Kathi and Becky can attest, kids come to this even more naturally than adults. One student Becky works with became fascinated with coding. A couple years after being introduced to MakeCode, he began coding inside Minecraft, using predesigned code that he would paste into the game to deliver a particular result. But he immediately wanted to know *why* the code produced those results. He scoured the block-based elements, looking for loops, logic statements, and block locations. He toggled to JavaScript, looking for things he could change to make the coding his own. It completely ignited an interest in coding within Minecraft that he hadn't shown before, and the activities caused him to grow in his critical thinking practices because he was interested in the artifact he was creating.

Get ready to set sail: Log in to Minecraft: Education Edition with your Office 365 account (if you don't have it installed already, visit aka.ms/download to get your copy). Create a new world, and press C to launch Code Builder. We recommend starting with a build tutorial, so you can get the hang of how your Agent works in the game. You can do this alongside your students as co-learners.

Conclusion

Dr. Michael Harvey is originally from New Zealand, but he teaches in Johor, Malaysia, just across the border from Singapore. Michael teaches advanced sciences, namely higher-level IB physics and chemistry, to secondary students. What sets Michael apart is his ability to communicate complicated concepts to his students such that they can think critically about them and communicate their thinking in turn. His lessons incorporate blended e-learning using augmented and virtual reality, digital portfolios, and the explanation of complex abstract scientific ideas through digital animations, which learners also co-create. He is quite gifted at embedding practical problem-based approaches through experiments into his lessons to reinforce critical thinking on the part of his students. Let's start by setting up what he does before introducing how he uses Microsoft Education tools.

> As a teacher of physics and chemistry, I love using Merge Cube (an augmented reality tool) to bring abstract models to life. My students can view a molecule when we're doing the lesson, so

they know what it looks like, and then they can create it. It works the same with cells—they can see it in their hands. It's quite powerful. The older students don't always see the practical application of this at first. They question, "Why are we doing this? What's the point?" But once they start using it, they say, "Oh, that's what it looks like! That's what you were talking about! Now I get it." On the whiteboard everything is in two dimensions, and you can't properly get a feel for the actual structures. With the Merge Cube, they can actually turn it around in their hand and observe it like never before.

I'm teaching the lessons and pointing out the parts and functions of various structures, but then I task them with creating it. They've got to prove to me that they actually understand what I'm talking about by creating the structures in three dimensions. The creation of these things is often happening in a program called CoSpaces, where we can build and design things in three dimensions that can then be viewed up close and from multiple angles by using these images in conjunction with the Merge Cubes. The advantage is that the students are creating it and then applying it through the Merge Cubes and their devices.

What's remarkable is how Michael then incorporates many Microsoft tools into his instruction. In doing so, he makes learning accessible, relevant, critical, and challenging for his students. As you read the rest of his story, think about the purpose behind each of these tools and the way it is used to support deeper thinking strategies.

I present the original lessons through OneNote pages, where I can embed these 3D models, but I'm also incorporating Flipgrid, so they have to explain what they know about the models using Flipgrid. They create informative videos that are three to four minutes long. There's this verbalization of what they're doing and learning, so they're ultimately learning to present as well.

That's important to me, because I want my students to be EAL (English as an Additional Language), so rather than having them write down things, which they struggle with, they can actually talk to the camera, so it's more natural for them. I can assess in that way too, by listening to their verbal explanation of what they have created.

I've had this one student in class who is not great at sitting down and focusing, so video is actually a very creative and useful way that he can express himself. Otherwise he just feels down because he loses concentration quite easily. He's had problems in other classes for that reason, so video is a very good way to assess his learning—particularly through Flipgrid, because he's not able to express what he's learned in other traditional ways. That's a success story.

I do flipped lessons as well, so basically all of my PowerPoints, which I present during the lessons, I translate into Japanese, Korean, and Chinese, because those are the major languages. I use Microsoft Translator to do that. I also record those PowerPoints, so students have access to the video if they're not there, and they can also play them again. I've taught my students how to use the Microsoft Translator tool when they need it. I had been using Sway as a presentation tool, but now that I've modeled it and students are using it, I'll have them creating with these tools too.

I'm also using Microsoft Whiteboard on my Surface as part of my teaching. Rather than me giving them feedback in class, I basically give them the exam question they got wrong, and then using the Surface, I annotate the answers. I give them the work example and the answers, and then I save that as a video. I can just annotate right on the screen, do a voiceover, and share with them the areas in which they need to improve.

It's all quite useful. All these Microsoft tools I've mentioned are ways I make learning accessible and engaging for my students, and they're able to do more critical thinking about the subjects and the content because of the way they are immersed in it.

Let's loop back to the definition of critical thinking that we started with at the beginning of this chapter: "the intellectually disciplined process of actively and skillfully conceptualizing, applying, analyzing, synthesizing, and/or evaluating information gathered from, or generated by, observation, experience, reflection, reasoning, or communication, as a guide to belief and action." Throughout this chapter, we have not just given examples of tools that can enable all of these rich, deep, and rigorous skills, but we have also provided phenomenal examples of educators from around the world who intentionally embed and expect critical thinking in their lessons. It is always the teachers that breathe meaning into the tools. They've left us with inspiration, allowing us to think critically about how we can use all those verbs up there to find ways to make critical thinking work in our own classrooms.

It is always the teachers that breathe meaning into the tools.

Critical and Computational Thinking Anchor Points

⚓ When you write your lesson objectives, be intentional about challenging students to think more deeply about the topic.

⚓ Diverse learners need to be exposed to a diverse set of tools and opportunities to learn how to select the right tool for the right situation to engage in critical thinking.

⚓ Organizational skills and executive functional skills are a huge part of being able to think critically. Use tools like OneNote, Immersive Reader, Office Lens, digital inking, and others mentioned in this chapter to purposefully foster these abilities and explicitly teach these skills with your students.

Crew Member Spotlights:
Sarah Clark and Nelly Hamed

Watch and listen as Sarah Clark from Scotland explains how her students use critical thinking skills.

Watch and listen as Nelly Hamed from Egypt explains how her students use computational thinking skills.

Sarah Clark

Nelly Hamed

Use your Flipgrid app to scan the QR codes for an augmented reality experience or use any QR code reader to view as a standard video. You can also access the link to this video from the Wakelet collection for this chapter.

Conclusion:
Becoming Changemakers

What a journey! In this book you have traveled the world with us to meet educators who are helping us welcome you into a wonderful global community. We have shared ways to communicate and collaborate with students and others. We have given a multitude of innovative examples for enhancing creativity in the classroom. Together we have contributed powerful ideas for getting students to think critically and computationally. We believe that the 7 Cs we celebrated in this book are paramount to enabling students (and all people) to become changemakers. In fact, we believe that Microsoft tools and programs are setting up conditions to enable our students to become global citizens who are not just capable but also compelled to actively change the world for the better. Of course, we have a few more stories to inspire you.

Helping Each Other: Changemaking with Skype in the Classroom

W

We are incredibly honored to know educators around the world, more than we could ever capture in a book, who are making changes in their schools and communities with few resources and a massive amount of endurance. Our colleague Oluwakemi Olurinola, for example, who lives in Nigeria, works with students all around the country to improve their access to technology and connect them with others around the world. As an educational technologist and Skype Master Teacher, Oluwakemi has traveled into rural communities to help students begin to break down their digital barriers to information.

> As an educator in a low-resource community, one of our low-cost but equally effective technology integration solutions is introducing Skype in the Classroom. This has given us the opportunity to engage with classroom and students across the globe, visiting places that would have been practically impossible but for Microsoft's Skype in the Classroom platform. Through video exchanges on Skype in the Classroom, my students and I embarked on learning about the world with the world. Living in a country challenged by inadequate technology infrastructure in schools and a lack of affordable internet connectivity, armed with just a laptop and a hotspot, I have been able to break down the classroom walls and connect students to classrooms across the globe. My reward is the delight on the faces of these students when they come to the realization during the connection that they are more alike than different from the kids in other parts of the world. This is the ultimate satisfaction I get from making these connections happen at all odds.

Armed with just a laptop and a hotspot, I have been able to break down the classroom walls and connect students to classrooms across the globe.

Our classroom connections have also yielded some memorable initiatives. On one connection, the classroom in Nigeria I aided in connecting with a class in the United States for a Mystery Skype call didn't have a world map. I hadn't realized this until the point of connection. So, we came up with the idea to guess each other's country codes instead of locations. We basically played a "guess my number" game. Mystery Number Skype came to be that day! It was such a great connection, but the beauty of that connection was that the classroom in the United States raised funds and bought the classroom in Nigeria world maps and the USA map too!

Another memorable Skype in the Classroom connection was in August 2017. I needed someone to connect virtually with the kids about any of the UN Sustainable Development Goals since they were being introduced to the topic. It was a last-minute call, and Manuela Correia stepped in to Skype with us on plastic waste and its effects on the environment. Manuela is a music teacher in Portugal with a passion for keeping our earth clean. That was how her Skype plastic clean-up brigade lessons/campaign started. Since her first call with us that summer, she has reached over 160 schools, and our connection again this summer made for her 225th class.

These are pointers to the ripple effects one Skype in the Classroom call can have, not just locally but globally. Being part of such a global community of educators not only broadened my horizon but also exposed me to global best practices as I connected with educators from across the globe, building a diverse and dynamic professional network of people who choose to make a difference.

This is one story of changemaking in one community that warms our hearts and fires our motivation to achieve more. You can be this teacher in your community! The art of teaching combined with the power of technology can change lives for students near and far and impact the future of our entire planet.

Going Global:
Changemaking Resources in the
Microsoft Educator Center

In September 2015, world leaders agreed to seventeen Sustainable Development Goals, which could mean an end to extreme poverty, inequalities, and climate change by 2030. The idea is that all countries need to incorporate study of these goals into their education system and their curricula. By teaching our youngest learners about the world's problems and issues, they can be part of the solution. Indeed, our youth may very well be the greatest part of our solution, and we need their help. Microsoft has fully embraced the need to teach the Sustainable Development Goals, and, in fact, has courses and resources on the Microsoft Educator Center so teachers and students around the world can educate themselves on ways to become the changemakers of the future—and the changemakers of now.

Jennifer Williams hails from Clearwater, Florida, USA, where she is a professor at Saint Leo University. Her zest for global change has led her to be a partner in the Innovation Lab Schools project, for which she is the Take Action Global Executive Director and lead instructional designer. In 2016, Jennifer joined forces with Ada McKim, Amy Rosenstein, and Fran Siracusa to identify ways to impact the world and stimulate action through education. Since then, she has immersed herself in nonprofit work to help build schools in refugee camps and remote areas of Africa, South America, and Asia. Jen has spoken to the United Nations about the need to incorporate instruction around the Sustainable Development Goals into education and continues to work with leaders and educators around the world to further this mission.

To exemplify her dedication to engage youth all over the world, Jen created a global project called the Goals Project. In her own words, this is how she summarizes this noble undertaking.

In September 2019, Amy Rosenstein and I launched our first Goals Project, hoping to get seventeen total global classrooms to participate. I was absolutely amazed when over fifteen hundred classrooms of students (over thirty thousand students) ages three years through university from over seventy countries joined together to explore the UN Sustainable Development Goals. For the project, classrooms were each assigned to one team with seventeen total age-level classrooms and then each assigned to one of the seventeen Global Goals. They were then guided through a four-week learning experience to create a project related to their goal. At the end of the month, classrooms were invited to share their creative projects with the larger group to teach about their assigned Sustainable Development Goal.

One of my very favorite parts of the entire project was that, for the students, it was led by Goals Project Student Ambassador Ayush Chopra! Ayush became a celebrity in the eyes of the participating students, showing them that student voice matters. Each week, he would kick off the learning with a short video, and for week 1, we invited them into a giant Goals Project virtual handshake using Flipgrid! In just a few weeks, we had thousands of videos created, almost sixty thousand views, and nearly five hundred hours of student engagement! You can view the entire video collection on Flipgrid.

At the conclusion of the project, to our great surprise, Flipgrid awarded us the #Flipgrid500 badge, naming us in the top five hundred Flipgrids of all time as global amplifiers (top five hundred in over one million Flipgrid educator accounts!)

Ayush concluded our project with this quote from Lao Tzu: "The journey of a thousand miles starts with one single step."

As of March 2020, the TeachSDGs Goals Project had four cohorts of teacher ambassadors, including sixteen hundred participating classrooms with over thirty thousand students worldwide. There are over thirty-five thousand teachers participating in the TeachSDGs organization!

In Jennifer's final Goals Project curated library of projects, you can watch videos and see the determination of students of all ages, from various countries and cultural backgrounds, from diverse classrooms in all corners of the world. All of these children did something to act for a better world. All of them had a month to learn about something that moved them, that stirred something inside of them to be bold and make a difference. All of them connected with others around the world through Flipgrid, Skype in the Classroom, and Sway, and they all shared their voices globally. These children and their voices are the hope for the future. These children are the changemakers.

Get ready to set sail: Follow @TeachSDGs on Twitter to become a part of this visionary global community. Then consider how you can involve your students in learning about the Sustainable Development Goals and how they can impact their own communities—and the world.

WE Can Make a Difference: Changemaking with WE.org

In this final chapter, we've shared an individual teacher story and a story of a teacher who created a global movement. We'd like to close with a way that you can be supported in your changemaking, a way that you can take action and be part of a group focused on changing lives through education.

WE.org is a global organization and Microsoft partner with a mission to "[m]ake doing good doable." Twenty-four years ago, founders **W** Craig Kielburger, Marc Kielburger, and Roxanne Joyal were bothered by the very notion of global poverty and decided to do something about it. What started as the mission of three has grown into a massive global community of changemakers. Their website and their organization do everything they can to empower youth and provide the tools for members of the global community to get involved and take action. You can sign up to become a WE School, participate in WE projects, or learn from others in the WE community.

Perhaps one of the most powerful components of WE.org is a series of events they host across Canada and the United States. These events are each called WE Day, and they are massive. For instance, at WE Day New York 2019 at Barclays Center on Long Island, seventeen thousand youth filled the massive sports stadium with energy. Students, teachers, and groups were there free of cost and by invitation only. The invitations were granted to changemakers who had applied by sharing the stories of the ways they were acting for a better world. There were groups that planted trees or did organized beach clean-ups, there were students who started anti-bullying campaigns, there were groups who created fundraisers to raise money for the hungry, there were school groups who initiated kindness campaigns, and there were children who connected with other children around the world to form larger communities to take on issues like climate change.

If you have a chance to attend a WE Day, you should. They are days of high-energy performances by television and radio celebrities, sports stars and legends, authors, political and historical leaders, and students who get up on the mega-stage to speak about the impacts they are making. Bring your tissues! During some of the stories, you'll need to dab an eye. There is so much goodness in our world, and WE Day is a celebration of the changemakers who create it. This is indeed a changemaker movement, and it aligns perfectly with Microsoft's mission statement "to empower every person and every organization on the planet to achieve more."

You might consider this conclusion an ending, but we think it's a beginning. It's a call to action for you and your students. We challenge you to embrace the 7 Cs as you continue your journey with Microsoft tools. Explore the suggested activities within this book, and reach out to us and the entire Microsoft Education community for help or to share your successes. We believe that each one of you have it within you to be—and to inspire—profound changemakers of the future.

Crew Member Spotlight: Oluwakemi Olurinola

Oluwakemi O.

Watch and listen as Oluwakemi Olurinola from Nigeria tells the story of changemaking happening in her community.

GETTING MORE INVOLVED WITH MICROSOFT EDUCATION

I f you're using Microsoft products, you've probably connected with Microsoft product teams in some way. You've likely received emails or contacted them for support. Perhaps you've noticed that their products all have a tab or area where you can get help or even give feedback. That's a great place to start, but when you're ready to really hop into the community, there are a whole bunch of people, places, and ideas to help you get connected.

- **The MEC:** The Microsoft Educator Center (education. microsoft.com) is often just called the MEC (məc). It's the main website for learning about everything Microsoft Education. You can watch quick videos about how to use products and features or share them with your students.

You can explore entire learning paths for a deeper dive into mastering Microsoft products. You can learn about products and organizations that have partnered with Microsoft. Best of all, you can take courses and earn points and collect badges for each course you take. The MEC keeps track of all your progress. Most people are motivated by the points and badges they earn, and they even post their successes to social media, where others in the community celebrate their progress.

- **Social Media:** Social media is a great way to stay connected, and it seems that Twitter is the frontrunner for a lot of the people involved in educational technology. Check out hashtags like #MicrosoftEdu, #MIEExpert, and #MSFTEduChat to connect with other community members. There are also Facebook groups, Pinterest pages, and even Wakelet collections to help you connect with information and people.

- **MIE, MIEExpert, MIETrainer, MIE Fellows, MCE, and MOS:** These are all different levels and certifications within the Microsoft Community. More information can be found in the MEC. Everyone, everywhere can become any of these things!

- **Microsoft Stores:** The Microsoft stores do so much more than sell products. They are also a great hub for learning, workshops, and meeting other Microsoft enthusiasts. If you're lucky enough to have a store nearby, stop in and see what's happening.

Fast Follows

Here's a list of the teachers and Microsoft team members we high-lighted who are active on Twitter. Twitter is a great way to connect with educators all over the world. If you're just getting started with Twitter, go follow some of our recommended Microsoft Education accounts as well. And of course, follow us!

Becky Keene—@beckykeene

Kathi Kersznowski—@kerszi

Microsoft Education

Microsoft Education—@MicrosoftEdu

Flipgrid—@Flipgrid

Microsoft Teams—@MicrosoftTeams

Minecraft: Education Edition—@PlayCraftLearn

OneNote for Education—@OneNoteEdu

Skype in the Classroom—@SkypeClassroom

Tweet Meet—@MSFTEduChat

Video Editor—@VideoEditorEdu

Changemakers

Amanda Calitz—@AmandaCalitz

Anna Dyagileva—@AnnaDyagileva1

Ayush Chopra–@AyushChopra24

Bonnie McClelland—@BMcClelland24

Cal Armstrong—@sig225

Dyane Smokorowski—@mrs_smoke

Emma Nääs—@emmanaas72

Felisa Ford—@APSITFeli

Ginny Grier—@BellsPrincipal

Gloria Enrique—@MissGEnrique

Hector Minto—@hminto

Jen Saarinen—@snej80

Jennifer Verschoor—@jenverschoor

Jennifer Williams—@JenWilliamsEdu

Jim Yanuzzelli—@jamesyanuzzelli

Julie Fletcher—@JulFletch

Kelli Etheredge—@ketheredge

Koen Timmers—@zelfstudie

Lanny Watkins—@lanny_watkins

Lee Whitmarsh—@l_whitmarsh

Luis Oliveira—@loliveira55

Manuela Correia—@litterasea1

Marija Petreska—@teachermarija

Marjolein Hoekstra—@MSEDUCentral

Meenoo Rami—@MeenooRami

Melanie LeJeune—@maclejeune

Michael Harvey—@dr_harves

Michelle Budge—@mdfriend

Mike Tholfsen—@mtholfsen

Mio Horio—@mibra_mio

Monika Limmer—@MonikaLimmer

Nelly Hamed—@nelly_hamed

Oluwakemi Olurinola—@kolurinola

Pauline Maas—@4pip

Prabhath Mannapperuma—@dprabhathm

Rachel Chisnall—@ibpossum

Sarah Clark—@sfm36

Scott Bricker—@BrickerCoaching

Stacey Ryan—@sryanalr

Stéphane Cloatre—@StephaneCloatre

Steve Auslander—@sauslander

Steve Isaacs—@mr_isaacs

Tammy Dunbar—@TammyDunbar

ACKNOWLEDGMENTS

We would like to thank all the educators who graciously shared their stories with us to help make this book possible. We also extend our appreciation to all the team members at Microsoft Education who connected us with new stories and experiences from around the world. We are so humbled to be a part of the global movement that is becoming the modern classroom, particularly through the lens of Microsoft's limitless learning tools.

Much love to my extended family, who supports my professional life and keeps me focused on what matters most at home. To my husband and children, thank you for being my constant cheerleaders, and to my parents, thank you for teaching me that anything is possible and to always #DreamBig. And to all the educators, leaders, students, and colleagues I have had in my twenty years in education, who have each supported, changed, and challenged me in a million ways: a simple thank you is never enough. My world shines in yellow because of you.

—Becky

It is with profound love and gratitude that I dedicate this book to my family. To Mom and Dad, you have given me the gifts of every-thing—life, a happy and enriched upbringing, and perpetual love. You've both given me a portion of yourselves, and I am infinitely grateful. If there is any goodness, strength, intelligence, talent, cre-ativity, empathy, or kindness within me, it is because it all came from you. You've always made me feel that I can do anything . . . so I wrote a book! Most of all, I always want to make both of you smile, to make you proud, and to be sure that you know I will eternally love you a bushel and a peck . . . and a hug around the neck! To the love of my life, Matt, I adore you. You believe in me more than I believe in myself, you clear pathways to make everything possible, you are my one true love, and there is no place I'd rather be than in your arms. Together, the world is our oyster. Thank you for reeling me in and loving me—hook, line, and sinker! You are my dreams, my best friend, my greatest catch, and my everything, and I love you . . . forever and more. To my son, Ryan, you are truly the most incredible human being I have ever known. Know that through the years as my Schoochie baby, my 'Sponsible boy, my fishing fanatic, and my University of Tampa student, you have brought so much joy! Thank you for being the perfect son always, for your generous and kind heart, for being proud of your ol' mom, and for making me a better person through your example. You make me endlessly proud.

—Kathi

ABOUT THE AUTHORS

Becky Keene's current role is Director of Content and Professional Learning for insight2execution, a Microsoft Global Training Partner and vendor based in Redmond, Washington. She works as a project manager for content development for worldwide edtech companies and also manages i2e's professional learning specialists and training engagements with major school systems around the United States.

Previously, Becky spent almost a decade as a One-to-One Program Specialist for Kent School District in Kent, Washington. In this role, she supported, trained, coached, and advocated for teachers across the district in the area of technology integration, specifically for Kent's 1:1 laptop initiative. As a pilot classroom teacher for 1:1 in 2005, she was recognized by the *Wall Street Journal*, NBC World News, and Comcast Newsmakers. Becky's classroom teaching experience is at the elementary and middle-school levels (ages eight to fourteen). She holds a master's degree in Elementary Literacy and is proud to be a National Board-Certified Teacher, Microsoft Education Master Trainer, and Microsoft Certified Educator.

Becky has been a top request to lead and speak at both regional and international events for Microsoft in Education. She has presented about best practices in technology education for the International Society of Technology Education; the Anytime, Anywhere Learning Foundation; the One-to-One Institute; the National School Board Association; and the Northwest Council for Computer Education.

She focuses her own professional growth on learning new things and expanding her practices by holding a position as Director of Amazing Things with a games-based learning startup Phygital Labs and by actively engaging with the educator community for tools she loves as a Microsoft Innovative Educator Expert, Minecraft Global Mentor, Flipgrid Student Voice Global Ambassador, and champion for OneNote, Wakelet, Peardeck, Genially, Buncee, and Novel Effect. Becky is also the co-founder of the professional book club HookEd, which includes cohorts of readers from around the world discussing education-centric books at quarterly virtual meet-ups. Most importantly, Becky is a wife and mom who loves to train for triathlons, water ski and snow ski, read books, and eat popcorn. Connect with her at beckykeene.com or on Twitter @beckykeene.

Kathi Kersznowski is currently a passionate leader and Technology Integration Specialist at Washington Township Public Schools in New Jersey, where she says that the very best part of her job is the people that she serves—the teachers! Kathi is also proud to work for a premiere Microsoft Global Training Partner called insight2execution (i2e) as a Professional Learning Specialist. Additionally, she is the owner of an Educational Technology Consulting business called Integration Innovation, LLC. She is a blogger, a keynote speaker, and a global presenter on various educational technology, STEM/STEAM, and leadership topics. In her past career lives, Kathi has worked as an elementary teacher, a special education teacher, and a computer teacher, and she even holds a master's degree in School Administration . . . which she hasn't actually used—yet!

Kathi is a voracious lifelong learner. In addition to being a proud MIEExpert, Microsoft Master Trainer, Minecraft Certified Trainer, and Skype Master Teacher, Kathi is an ambassador for several popular edtech companies, including Flipgrid, Wakelet, Merge, Buncee, Empatico, Genially, Novel Effect, Seesaw, and the #TeachSDGs movement. In 2019, Kathi was awarded Flipgrid's highest honor: Student Voice Champion of the Year. She can often be found fervently interacting on Twitter, attending edcamps on weekends, reading blogs, catching webinars, being a guest on podcasts, attending education conferences just for fun, and even organizing local coffee meet-ups to have a chance to chat with other fun educators.

Kathi is the creator of the original #LearningInTheLoo movement globally, and she's also the creator of some Flipgrid-themed favorites you may know: #Fliphunt, #FlipmojiScenes, and the inaugural #Flipathon.

When she remembers to focus on that "life" part of "work/life balance," Kathi most enjoys traveling with her husband, Matt, and son, Ryan, fairly often to Florida where her parents live. She also just loves a cozy bonfire, being out in nature, drinking really strong coffee and lots of it, doing a little saltwater fishing and crabbing, baking up a storm, going out for a flight, planning new vacation adventures, reading nonfiction mysteries, taking long Jeep drives with the roof off, slurping down some raw oysters, tent camping, kayaking, taking too many photos, and enjoying ridiculously long midday naps. Connect with Kathi on Twitter @kerszi.

SPEAKING

Becky Keene and Kathi Kersznowski are both available to speak about Sailing the 7 Cs with Microsoft in Education and can share examples from this book aligned with the 7 Cs model with your audience. Interested parties can reach out to Becky and Kathi individually, as they offer different perspectives and backgrounds that may best target your needs.

Becky has been a keynote speaker and professional development facilitator across the United States and across four continents (her goal is to reach all six inhabited continents; help her out!). She has trained and inspired thousands of educators and school leaders around the world. Her background in and passion for modern education, instructional technology, quality professional development, system change management, empowering students, and games-based learning shines when she speaks. Ask her to speak at your event by contacting her directly through her website: beckykeene.com.

Becky's favorite topics include but are not limited to the following:

- Creating an inclusive classroom
- Games-based learning
- Empowering student voice
- How to make change contagious
- Social-emotional learning and its impact on education
- Integrating computational thinking
- Modern professional learning practices
- Innovative assessment strategies
- Microsoft tools in your classroom
- Appsmashing Office 365

Kathi has also been a keynote speaker, professional development provider, and workshop presenter—but only on three continents so far! She began presenting years ago on the local edcamp circuit, graduated to education conferences throughout her state, then began presenting nationally at renowned conferences such as TCEA and ISTE, and eventually was asked to present several times in Europe at the famous BETT conference in London, and in Australia at a prestigious Microsoft event known as E2.

Kathi has been named one of the 100 NJ Educators to Follow on Twitter, has been featured on the Women in Education Leadership podcast, was interviewed about Microsoft's Learning Tools for the #Edtechchat podcast, was featured on the Ditch That Textbook podcast speaking about #Fliphunt, contributed to #EdtechStories podcast about Wakelet, was featured on the Flipgrid Voice Rockstar blog and in their film festival, was interviewed for the DisruptED TV broadcast, and was quoted in the Edvocate's "106 Experts Share Their Thoughts on the Future of Education". Kathi is a former district Teacher of the Year. She has been published in *ASCD Inservice*, *DisruptED Magazine*, *eSchoolNews*, and the *Edcamp Newsletter*.

Kathi is the founder of Edcamp Happy Camper. You can always reach Kathi on Twitter at @kerszi, or through her edtech consulting business, Integration Innovation, LLC, at IntegrationInnovation@gmail.com.

Kathi has shared her expertise by presenting about a variety of diverse topics related to educational technology, STEM, and educational leadership. Some of her favorite and most-requested topics include the following:

- Various specific websites and apps—the why and the how (e.g., Flipgrid, Buncee, Wakelet)
- Making the Most of Microsoft (various Microsoft applications)
- Purposeful and Relevant Technology Integration! It's a P.A.R.T.I.!
- Take the Leadership Leap!
- Technology and the School Administrator/Power Tools for School Administrators
- Trailblazing Leadership: 10 Steps for Establishing Yourself as a Leader
- The #1 Most Critical EdTech Investment You Can Make
- What Is a Technology Integration Specialist? I'll Teach You My 12-Part Success Model
- Take a Walk through My Tech-Infused Classroom
- EdTech: Reflecting on the Past, Preparing for the Future
- Awesome Apps—and Ways to Integrate Them (a hands-on, task-based experience)
- Bring Learning to Life with Augmented Reality in the Classroom
- The Making of a Makerspace: Getting Started and Getting Organized
- Developing Global Citizens and Future-Ready Students
- Digital Tools to Amplify Student Voices
- Global Learning: It Makes a World of Difference

MORE FROM

DAVE BURGESS
Consulting, inc.

Since 2012, DBCI has been publishing books that inspire and equip educators to be their best. For more information on our titles or to purchase bulk orders for your school, district, or book study, visit **DaveBurgessconsulting.com/DBCIbooks**.

More Technology & Tools

50 Things You Can Do with Google Classroom by Alice Keeler and Libbi Miller

50 Things to Go Further with Google Classroom by Alice Keeler and Libbi Miller

140 Twitter Tips for Educators by Brad Currie, Billy Krakower, and Scott Rocco

Block Breaker by Brian Aspinall

Code Breaker by Brian Aspinall

Google Apps for Littles by Christine Pinto and Alice Keeler

Master the Media by Julie Smith

Reality Bytes by Christine Lion-Bailey, Jesse Lubinsky, Micah Shippee, PhD

Shake Up Learning by Kasey Bell

Social LEADia by Jennifer Casa-Todd

Stepping Up to Google Classroom by Alice Keeler and Kimberly Mattina

Teaching Math with Google Apps by Alice Keeler and Diana Herrington

Teachingland by Amanda Fox and Mary Ellen Weeks

Like a PIRATE™ Series

Teach Like a PIRATE by Dave Burgess
eXPlore Like a Pirate by Michael Matera
Learn Like a Pirate by Paul Solarz
Play Like a Pirate by Quinn Rollins
Run Like a Pirate by Adam Welcome

Lead Like a PIRATE™ Series

Lead Like a PIRATE by Shelley Burgess and Beth Houf
Balance Like a Pirate by Jessica Cabeen, Jessica Johnson, and
     Sarah Johnson
Lead beyond Your Title by Nili Bartley
Lead with Appreciation by Amber Teamann and Melinda Miller
Lead with Culture by Jay Billy
Lead with Instructional Rounds by Vicki Wilson
Lead with Literacy by Mandy Ellis
     Leadership & School Culture
Culturize by Jimmy Casas
Escaping the School Leader's Dunk Tank by Rebecca Coda and
     Rick Jetter
From Teacher to Leader by Starr Sackstein
The Innovator's Mindset by George Couros
It's OK to Say "They" by Christy Whittlesey
Kids Deserve It! by Todd Nesloney and Adam Welcome
Live Your Excellence by Jimmy Casas
Let Them Speak by Rebecca Coda and Rick Jetter
The Limitless School by Abe Hege and Adam Dovico
Next-Level Teaching by Jonathan Alsheimer
The Pepper Effect by Sean Gaillard
The Principled Principal by Jeffrey Zoul and Anthony McConnell
Relentless by Hamish Brewer
The Secret Solution by Todd Whitaker, Sam Miller, and
     Ryan Donlan
Start. Right. Now. by Todd Whitaker, Jeffrey Zoul, and Jimmy Casas
Stop. Right. Now. by Jimmy Casas and Jeffrey Zoul

They Call Me "Mr. De" by Frank DeAngelis

Unmapped Potential by Julie Hasson and Missy Lennard

Word Shift by Joy Kirr

Your School Rocks by Ryan McLane and Eric Lowe

Teaching Methods & Materials

All 4s and 5s by Andrew Sharos

Boredom Busters by Katie Powell

The Classroom Chef by John Stevens and Matt Vaudrey

The Collaborative Classroom by Trevor Muir

Copyrighteous by Diana Gill

Ditch That Homework by Matt Miller and Alice Keeler

Ditch That Textbook by Matt Miller

Don't Ditch That Tech by Matt Miller, Nate Ridgway, and
    Angelia Ridgway

EDrenaline Rush by John Meehan

Educated by Design by Michael Cohen, The Tech Rabbi

The EduProtocol Field Guide by Marlena Hebern and Jon Corippo

The EduProtocol Field Guide: Book 2 by Marlena Hebern and
    Jon Corippo

Instant Relevance by Denis Sheeran

LAUNCH by John Spencer and A.J. Juliani

Make Learning MAGICAL by Tisha Richmond

Pure Genius by Don Wettrick

The Revolution by Darren Ellwein and Derek McCoy

Shift This! by Joy Kirr

Skyrocket Your Teacher Coaching by Michael Cary Sonbert

Spark Learning by Ramsey Musallam

Sparks in the Dark by Travis Crowder and Todd Nesloney

Table Talk Math by John Stevens

The Wild Card by Hope and Wade King

The Writing on the Classroom Wall by Steve Wyborney

Inspiration, Professional Growth & Personal Development

Be REAL by Tara Martin

Be the One for Kids by Ryan Sheehy

The Coach ADVenture by Amy Illingworth

Creatively Productive by Lisa Johnson

Educational Eye Exam by Alicia Ray

The EduNinja Mindset by Jennifer Burdis

Empower Our Girls by Lynmara Colón and Adam Welcome

Finding Lifelines by Andrew Grieve and Andrew Sharos

The Four O'Clock Faculty by Rich Czyz

How Much Water Do We Have? by Pete and Kris Nunweiler

P Is for Pirate by Dave and Shelley Burgess

A Passion for Kindness by Tamara Letter

The Path to Serendipity by Allyson Apsey

Sanctuaries by Dan Tricarico

The SECRET SAUCE by Rich Czyz

Shattering the Perfect Teacher Myth by Aaron Hogan

Stories from Webb by Todd Nesloney

Talk to Me by Kim Bearden

Teach Better by Chad Ostrowski, Tiffany Ott, Rae Hughart, and Jeff Gargas

Teach Me, Teacher by Jacob Chastain

TeamMakers by Laura Robb and Evan Robb

Through the Lens of Serendipity by Allyson Apsey

The Zen Teacher by Dan Tricarico

Children's Books

Beyond Us by Aaron Polansky

Cannonball In by Tara Martin

Dolphins in Trees by Aaron Polansky

I Want to Be a Lot by Ashley Savage

The Princes of Serendip by Allyson Apsey

The Wild Card Kids by Hope and Wade King

Zom-Be a Design Thinker by Amanda Fox

CPSIA information can be obtained
at www.ICGtesting.com
Printed in the USA
BVHW041719070422
633694BV00009B/178